Football Crazy!

Compiled by Jimmy Hill

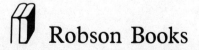 Robson Books

Designed and illustrated by Steve Lockett

First published in the United Kingdom in 1985 by
Robson Books Ltd., Bolsover House, 5-6 Clipstone Street,
London W1P 7EB. Copyright © 1985 Jimmy Hill

British Library Cataloguing in Publication Data

Hill, Jimmy
    Football crazy.
    1. Soccer
    I. Title
    796.334   GV943

    ISBN 0-86051-356-4

Printed in the United Kingdom by St Edmundsbury Press,
Bury St Edmunds, Suffolk.

Introduction

As someone who has had the good luck to see football from almost every angle (I've been a player, a manager and am now a television commentator), you will have to forgive my natural bias for saying that it is the most absorbing of games. It has been my pleasure and privilege to have shared in and witnessed a good many of the memorable episodes catalogued here — if only by virtue of being someone who has been fascinated with the game all his life. Football crazy? Yes, I probably am, but I hope it is not without reason.

Reason, too, cautions me against what seems to be the inevitable tendency we have of becoming a nation of watchers rather than players. This can be damaging, particularly for the young. By 'watchers', I refer largely to those who get their sport from television: it is a marvellous medium, in its place and viewed selectively — but if 'watching' results in our becoming physically lazy, it is far from being a blessing.

Add to this the scarcity of suitable facilities, and you have two reasons why young people do not become actively involved in sport. The magnetism of television (and now video, of course) coupled with the lack of opportunity, or even of invitation in some cases, mean that there is little incentive for them to get involved with football or any other kind of sport. That is why the work of the National Playing Fields Association and the Goaldiggers Trust is so vital. If those who have enjoyed a wide experience of sport in their lives can kindle a spark of enthusiasm in the young, the first challenge they must be prepared to meet is that of the sort of facilities they can offer. We really should try to ensure that all young people have the opportunity to play under reasonably decent circumstances, no matter what sport they want to try.

No less important is the question of harnessing the energy of the young into worthwhile channels. If you can do that, it solves the problem of the same energy being directed to worthless and unproductive ends — and ultimately, by a bitter irony in the case of football, into the sort of behaviour that has given the British game its current tragic reputation.

The provision of the right facilities for sport is a very positive way of making a valuable contribution to society, as well as to everyone who values the chance of enjoying the fun that can be had from physical exercise against an opponent, a result at the end of a game, and perhaps the opportunity to celebrate the victory, or defeat, with a small glass of something or other.

I hope this collection of fascinating football facts and anniversaries will help stimulate greater interest in the positive, active benefits of the game. The National Playing Fields Association and the Goaldiggers Trust deserve all our support — if only to make us football crazy in the best possible sense!

Kick-off

One January date from the whole of my football career sticks in my mind — 18 January 1961 was the day when professional players succeeded in getting the 'maximum wage' lifted. Until that momentous date we were seen by many people as almost half-criminals if we took more than twenty pounds a week, which was a ridiculous situation for declared professionals. Looking back, it seems incredible that that was the norm. Many people might argue that today the pendulum has swung the other way, but that is another matter.

At the time I was playing with Fulham, and I was also chairman of the Professional Footballers' Association. I remember thinking that it was quite frightening to be taking on our employers, although the negotiations and the fairly extensive television and press coverage proved to be very valuable to me as my career developed in the wider field of football.

That Wednesday in January was an historic moment, and I know that I can never hope to achieve anything like it again. In a sense, the serfs had changed their status to free men. The breakthrough that we achieved seemed like an impossible dream when the campaign began, for footballers had honestly thought they were going to be limited to a maximum wage for the rest of their days. In my case, however, it was poetic justice that this was to be my last year as a player, and so I never had the opportunity to negotiate a contract. I then turned to managing, and was on the paying end!

January

During a Division IV match against Aldershot on New Year's Day 1966 Chester had the misfortune to lose both full-backs, Ray Jones and Bryn Jones (no relation), with broken legs.

The only World Cup competition in which all four British home countries competed in the finals was the one held in Sweden in 1958.

It was not until the 1969/70 season that all 92 League clubs entered the Football League Cup.

1949 got off to a groggy start for Exeter City. With many of the team suffering from food poisoning, their trainer, J. Gallagher, found himself playing centre-half in their first match of the year against Norwich.

Jim Dyet of King's Park scored eight goals on his club debut against Forfar Athletic on 2 January 1930.

In 1982 Chris Garland joined Bristol City for the fourth time.

When Aston Villa became Division I champions in 1980/81 they called on a record number of only fourteen players, which included seven players who had played in every match (Jimmy Rimmer, Ken Swain, Ken McNaught, Des Bremner, Gordon Cowans, Dennis Mortimer and Tony Morley).

Jimmy Turnbull, Manchester United's Scottish centre-forward, was sent off in consecutive matches in 1909.

Pat Kruse of Torquay United made an unhappy entry into the record books on 3 January 1977 when he headed the ball into his own net a mere six seconds after kick-off in a match against Cambridge United.

Dave Watson is the only player to have been capped for England while playing for five different clubs (Sunderland, Manchester City, Werder Bremen, Southampton and Stoke City).

In 1972/73 Alfie Conn won a Scottish Cup winners' medal with Rangers after their victory over Celtic. Four years later he won another Scottish Cup winners' medal, this time playing for Celtic in their victory over Rangers.

John Ayteo, who played a record 597 games for Bristol City, played two Football League games for Portsmouth.

In their Division III (North) match against Accrington Stanley on 4 January 1930 all three Chesterfield half-backs, H. Wass, H. Wightman and R. Duckworth, scored goals.

The largest football stadium in the British Isles is Hampden Park, the home of Queen's Park, whose gate seldom exceeds 1,000. However, in 1937 Hampden Park accommodated 145,547 spectators for an international between Scotland and England.

Trevor Francis was involved in three £1 million transfers, and Nottingham Forest, who bought him from Birmingham in 1979, were involved in five. In addition to the Francis deal, they bought Ian Wallace from Coventry and Justin Fashanu from Norwich, sold Gary Birtles to Manchester United in 1980 and a year later sold Trevor Francis to Manchester City.

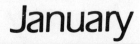

On 5 January 1935 Eddie Hapgood of Arsenal headed a goal from the rebound of his own penalty kick when it was fisted back to him by Riley, the Liverpool goalkeeper.

The third round of the FA Cup in the 1962/63 season was due to begin on 5 January, but because of appalling weather that winter there were 261 postponements and the final matches in the round were not played until 11 March.

Only four European countries competed in the first World Cup competition held in Uruguay in 1930. The three-week boat trip to South America discouraged all but France, Belgium, Yugoslavia and Romania from taking part.

In the dying minutes of the 1971 clash between Rangers and Celtic at Ibrox Park, Colin Stein scored an equalizer that set the match ablaze. Fans who were leaving the ground tried to get back up the steep terraces to see the closing stages and at Staircase 13 this resulted in tragedy when sixty-six people died in the resulting chaos, as those leaving surged against those trying to climb back up. In spite of the Bradford fire tragedy in May 1985, this still remains the highest crowd death toll at a British football ground.

While their ground was under suspension in 1921 Stockport were forced to play one of their Division III (North) games at Old Trafford, where only 200 people turned up to watch.

Since becoming founder members of Division III (North) in 1921 Hartlepool United and Crewe have opposed each other every season in the Football League except 1963/64.

On 5 January 1935 Eddie Hapgood headed a goal from the rebound of his own penalty kick.

Goal nets were patented by J.A. Brodie of Liverpool in 1890 and were first used in a North–South match at Nottingham on 7 January 1891.

In the 1927/28 season Nelson lost all twenty-one of their Division III (North) games.

In 1885 Birmingham City, formerly Small Heath, was the first Football League club to become a limited company.

In the summer of 1974 England kept a clean sheet for three successive international matches: East Germany, Bulgaria and Yugoslavia all failed to score against the team of R. Clemence, E. Hughes, A. Lindsay, C. Todd, D. Watson, M. Dobson, K. Keegan, M. Channon, F. Worthington, C. Bell and T. Brooking.

The birthday of Ted MacDougall, the only player to be the leading goal-scorer in three separate divisions: Division IV for Bournemouth in 1970/71; Division III for Bournemouth in 1971/72; and Division I for Norwich in 1975/76.

All seven clubs who have lost their League status since the Second World War have come from the north. The last southern club to lose its League status was Thames in the 1931/32 season.

Wembley Stadium was built in 1922 for £750,000, less than transfer fees paid in recent years for a single class player. A quarter of a million tons of clay had to be dug out to create the bowl of the stadium and the construction required the use of 25,000 tons of concrete, 600 tons of reinforcing rods, 1,500 tons of steel girders and 500,000 rivets used to build the stands.

9

On 9 January 1954 fifteen out of thirty-two FA Cup third-round ties resulted in draws.

On 9 January 1931 Dixie Dean's daughter was born, and Everton beat Southport 9–1 in an FA Cup quarter-final; the little girl was named Nina!

In 1967 Millwall had a winning run of fifty-nine home games at the Den before eventually losing a match to Plymouth.

In the 1946/47 season Doncaster Rovers won eighteen out of twenty-four away matches.

John Wark scored a hat-trick of penalties in Ipswich's 5–1 victory over Aris Salonika in the 1980/81 UEFA Cup.

10

In January 1981 Uruguay staged a tournament to commemorate fifty years of the World Cup. All former winners (with the exception of England, who were replaced by the Netherlands) were invited. The final was played on 10 January between the hosts and Brazil, the fiftieth meeting between the two countries, and was kicked off by Nestor Mascheroni, the only survivor of the 1930 final. Uruguay won 2–1 and collected the Copa de Oro (Gold Cup) designed by the Uruguayan artist Lincoln Presno. Their manager, Roque Gaston Mastopoli, had played as goalkeeper in the 1950 side.

In 1969 Torquay United drew eight consecutive matches.

Maurice Owen, a former Chindit in Burma under Orde Wingate, played for his local team, Abingdon, after being demobbed and was signed by Swindon in December 1946. On 11 January 1947 he made his debut for his new club and celebrated by scoring a hat-trick.

In the 1924/25 season Albert Chandler scored in each of sixteen Football League games for Leicester City in Division II.

Wally Ardron is the only player to have been leading scorer in both Division III (North) and Division III (South). While playing for Rotherham he scored twenty-nine goals in the 1948/49 season and in 1950/51 he scored thirty-six goals for Notts Forest in Division III (South).

Spurs were the first British club to win a major European competition when they won the European Cup-winners' Cup in 1963.

12

On 12 January 1963 the Football League programme was devastated by the weather. Only four out of the scheduled forty-four games were played that day, though north of the border things were marginally better with eight out of fifteen Scottish League and Cup games going ahead as planned.

In the 1937/38 season Brechin City suffered three 0–10 defeats.

Exeter City Football Club was formed in 1908 from an amalgamation of Exeter City and St Sidwell United.

In the ranks of professional football Ron Atkinson can claim honours at both Oxford and Cambridge. As a player he guided Oxford from Division IV to Division II, and as a manager he helped Cambridge to become Division III champions.

On 13 January 1923 non-League Worksop were drawn to play Spurs in the first round of the FA Cup. Spurs had won the Cup two years earlier and had been Division I runners-up the previous season; Worksop was urged to take the local cricket scorer to the game. However, he was not needed and at the end of the game Worksop had held Spurs to a 0–0 draw, to everyone's astonishment. The replay two days later was a different story; Spurs won 9–0 at White Hart Lane.

Charles Fowerraker managed Bolton Wanderers for twenty years between the two World Wars.

In 1970 Liverpool's full-back Chris Lawler scored ten goals from open play.

The Northampton cricketer 'Fanny' Waldron scored six goals in an Olympic Games match played in 1912.

When Arsenal arrived at Walsall on 14 January 1933 they were six points clear at the top of Division I, having beaten Sheffield United 9–2. Walsall's form from their last four matches had been three draws and a 0–5 defeat. Although Arsenal were playing without Hapgood, John, Lambert and Coleman, no one suspected the shock that was to follow: goals by Alsop and Sheppard gave Walsall victory and put Arsenal out of the Cup.

Stranraer is the only League Club in the world that is over 115 years old and has never had a player capped.

After their relegation in 1912/13 Arsenal dropped the name Woolwich at the instigation of a Fulham M.P. who was also responsible for their move to Highbury.

A Third Round FA Cup tie on 15 January 1972 seemed to end a fortnight of controversy at Manchester United and sank Southampton's cup hopes that season. Frank O'Farrell, the Manchester United manager, had dropped George Best from the previous week's League match for missing training. Against Southampton, however, Best put on a dazzling performance, culminating in a selfless dummy that led to the equalizing goal that forced a replay. Two months earlier Best had scored a hat-trick against Southampton in a League match.

Alex Stepney was a Chelsea footballer for 112 days in 1960. Having been bought from Millwall for £50,000 he was then sold to Manchester United after playing for Chelsea just once.

In 1972 Mansfied Town failed to score in their first nine Football League games.

King Carol of Romania, a keen football fan, selected the 1930 Romanian World Cup squad himself and even pardoned all outstanding football offences.

In the 1962/63 season three Brentford players scored sixty-seven goals in the Football League. All three were internationals, but not one won an international cap while playing for Brentford. J. Dick (who scored twenty-three goals) played once for England against Scotland in 1959 while he was with West Ham. J. Brooks (twenty-two goals) played three times for England in 1957, when he was with Spurs. And W. McAdams (twenty-two goals) played fifteen times for Northern Ireland from 1954 to 1962 while he was with Manchester City, Bolton and Leeds.

F. Roberts of Glentoran scored ninety-six goals for the Northern Irish club in the 1930/31 season, a record in British football.

On 16 January 1932, during the second-half of a match between Lincoln City and Halifax Town, Frank Keetley scored six goals in twenty-one minutes.

In 1926/27 George Camsell scored fifty-nine Division II goals for Middlesbrough including a record eight hat-tricks.

David Jack, who became the first player to be transferred for £10,000 when he moved from Bolton to Arsenal in 1928, had the middle names of Bone Nightingale.

At the end of the season in 1955 Birmingham City became the only Football League club to win a championship on goal average more than once. In 1920/21 they became Division II champions, beating Cardiff, with fifty-eight points and in 1954/55 they beat Luton Town and Rotherham with fifty-four points.

Twenty-two goals were scored in Sheffield on 17 January 1891 in two separate FA Cup ties. Sheffield Wednesday beat Halliwell 12–0 and Sheffield United lost to Notts County 1–9.

Fred Le May, who played for Thames, Clapton Orient and Watford between 1930 and 1933, was reputed to be the smallest Football League player at just five feet tall.

In 1931 Rochdale suffered thirteen consecutive home defeats.

Both the 1884 and 1885 FA Cup finals were contested by Blackburn Rovers and Queen's Park, and Blackburn won on both occasions.

Arsenal fielded three amateurs for their Division I match against Stoke in 1946 (Dr K. O'Flanagan, B. Joy and A. Goddmussen).

F. Howard made his League debut for Manchester City in their match against Liverpool on 18 January 1913. Playing at centre-forward he scored four goals in the course of the game.

Between 1939 and 1949 Bill McCandless managed three different teams that each earned promotion from Division III: Newport County in 1938/39, Cardiff City in 1946/47 and Swansea in 1948/49.

As manager of Chelsea in 1955 Ted Drake became the first man to both manage and play for Division I champions.

Frank and Hubert Heron are the only brothers to have appeared together in one season in an FA Cup final (for the Wanderers) and in an international. They achieved this feat in 1876.

Cardiff City achieved a unique treble on three consecutive Saturdays in 1924. On each occasion they beat Arsenal, winning 2–1 at Highbury in a Division I match on 19 January, 4–0 at Ninian Park the following week in another Division I game, and 1–0 on 2 February in the second round of the FA Cup, also played at Ninian Park.

England won the Olympic Games football titles in 1908 and 1912. Only V. Woodward and A. Berry played in both winning sides.

Gerry and Joe Baker both have the distinction of scoring nine or more goals in Scottish FA Cup matches: Gerry scored ten for St Mirren against Glasgow University in 1960 and Joe scored nine for Hibs in their match against Peebles Rovers in 1961.

I was chairman of the Professional Footballers' Association when we got the 'maximum wage' lifted on 18 January 1961, only three days before our threatened strike.

The first Football League match to be played on a Sunday took place at the Den on 20 January 1974 when Millwall beat Fulham 1-0 with a goal by Brian Clark.

England played their first Under-23 match on 20 January 1954 when they lost 0–3 to Italy at Bologna. However, they gained revenge the following year at Stamford Bridge with a 5–1 victory. Only Reg Matthews, Duncan Edwards and Frank Blunstone remained from the previous side.

Scunthorpe United was formed in 1904 and amalgamated with Lindsey United in 1910. It was not until 1951 that the name Lindsey was dropped from the club's name.

In 1888 the English Cup winners, West Brom, played the Scottish Cup winners, Renton, for the title Champions of the World — Renton won.

Following demands for increased wages in 1960, players issued a threat to strike on 21 January 1961 which would have brought the game to a halt until the Football League agreed to a number of concessions, the most important of which was the abolition of a maximum wage.

Port Vale's Roy Sproson, who played 755 Football League games for the club between 1950/51 and 1970/71, became the first holder of the Gillette award for the Sportsman of the Season in 1970.

Scotland's Gordon Smith played for three different Scottish League clubs in the European Cup: Hibs in 1956, Dundee in 1962 (both reaching the semi-finals) and Hearts in 1961.

The first Football League match to be broadcast was played at Highbury between Arsenal and Sheffield United on 22 January 1927.

The County Youth Cup was held for the first time in 1946 when Staffordshire were the winners.

The US team at the first World Cup finals in 1930 contained many Scottish immigrants who, thanks to their muscular appearance, were nicknamed 'the shotputters' by the French team.

The Welsh international Dai Davies is the only man to have played rugby league and association football at international level. He achieved this between 1904 and 1908.

Billy Bremner's birthday.

Chelsea's George Hildson scored five goals on his Football League debut on the opening day of the 1906/07 season in a match against Glossop North End.

Alex Villaplane, captain of the French team in the first World Cup competition in 1930, was executed fourteen years later, after the Liberation, for collaborating with the occupying Germans.

Since the change of the rule governing offsides in 1925, the record run of League matches played without conceding a goal is thirty, achieved by Port Vale in the 1953/54 season when they were Division III (North) champions and also reached the semi-final of the FA Cup.

24 January 1955 marked the end of a third-round FA Cup tie between Stoke City and Bury when Stoke finally beat their opponents 3–2. They had met on four previous occasions during the month and victory came after a total of nine hours and twenty-two minutes of play, the most protracted cup tie in British soccer.

Celtic's G. Connelly was the first substitute used by a British club in a European Cup final against Feyenoord in 1970.

In 1972 Francis Lee broke the record for the greatest number of penalties in a single season with a tally of thirteen.

By reaching the semi-finals of the League Cup in 1975 Chester became the last Division IV club to do so. That year the final was played by two Division II sides, Norwich and Aston Villa, making Manchester United the only Division I side to reach the semi-finals.

The great Portuguese international, Eusebio, was born Eusebio Da Sila Ferreira on 25 January 1942 in Lourenço Marques (now Maputo), Mozambique.

The Portuguese FA closed down Benfica's Stadium of Light for eight weeks following crowd trouble at a match against Belenenses on 25 January 1970. Benfica were a goal down and, with Torres sent off, the crowd invaded the pitch attacking players, the referee and officials.

In the 1880s Queen's Park went unbeaten for a run of seven years and for five of them their goalkeeper Jock Grant did not concede a goal.

In 1890 Sunderland became the first club to have points deducted for fielding an illegal player.

The semi-final played on 26 January 1972 between Stoke City and West Ham in the League Cup competition will probably be best remembered as the time when Bobby Moore, playing in goal, almost saved a penalty. The tie had started on 8 December 1971 at Stoke, when West Ham won 2-1; the second leg at Upton Park saw Stoke pull back that goal and the first play-off resulted in a goal-less draw at Hillsborough. The fourth match had been running thirteen minutes when Stoke's Terry Conroy collided with West Ham's goalkeeper, Bobby Ferguson and Ron Greenwood decided that Moore should deputize. Then West Ham's full-back, John McDowell, conceded a penalty. Bernard kicked from the penalty spot, Moore smothered the shot but was unable to hold on to the ball and Bernard put it in the net on the rebound. West Ham then scored twice; Ferguson resumed his position. Dobing equalized for Stoke and Terry Conroy clinched their place in the final with the goal that gave them a 3-2 victory. A total of 171,334 spectators had watched the four enthralling games.

1973/74 was the first season when three teams were promoted or relegated in the first three divisions. Southampton, Manchester United and Norwich City were relegated from Division I; Middlesbrough, Luton and Carlisle were promoted from Division II; Crystal Palace, Preston and Swindon were relegated from Division II and Oldham, Bristol Rovers and York were promoted from Division III.

Bobby Collins, who captained Leeds to win Division II in 1963/64, also captained Bury to win promotion to Division II in 1968, when they were runners-up to Oxford United in Division III.

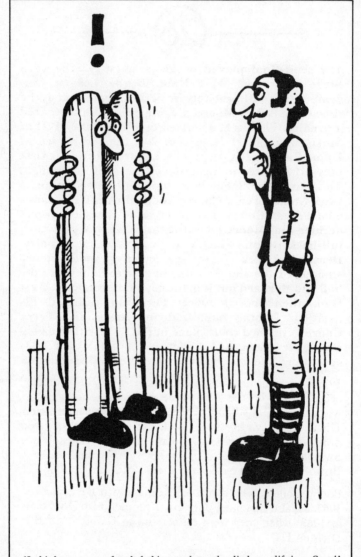

'I think your new-fangled shinguards need a little modifying, Sam!'

A 1-1 draw between Manchester City and Newcastle United on 27 January 1912 might have been a 4-1 victory for City if they had not missed a record three penalties during the game: Fletcher had a go at taking two and Thornlet fared no better with his one penalty.

Cardiff City, winners of the FA Cup in 1927, were bottom of Division III only seven seasons later.

In January 1965 Stanley Matthews became the first professional footballer to receive a knighthood; at the time he was still a registered player.

In 1939 Wolves became the first team to be runners-up in both the FA Cup and Division I in the same year. This fate awaited Burnley in 1962, Leeds in 1965 and Leeds again in 1970.

Watford signed five players from Leicester on 28 January 1948: Calvert, Eggleston, Cheney, Osborne and Hartley.

Berwick Rangers, the one Scottish League club in England, provided a major upset in the 1967 Scottish FA cup competition when they beat Glasgow Rangers 1-0 on 28 January with a goal scored by Sammy Reid. At that time Berwick were managed by Jock Wallace who later went on to become manager of Rangers.

Bolton Wanderers left-back John Slater was later MP for Eastbourne.

N.C. Bailey was the first England right-back and hence was nicknamed 'Prince of the half-backs'.

The British international Sam Widdowson, who played League Football for Nottingham Forest, is credited with the invention of shinguards in 1874.

There was a major upset in the 1949 FA Cup on 29 January when non-League Yeovil Town beat Sunderland. Thanks in no small measure to the notorious Yeovil Slope, their player manager Alec Stock scored an equalizer and an overhead kick that went wrong by Sunderland's Len Shackleton gave Yeovil victory.

One of football's unluckiest prodigies was Alick Jeffrey who made his Football League debut for Doncaster Rovers against Fulham when he was fifteen in the 1954/55 season. In 1955 he played once for the England Youth team and two years later twice for the England Under-23 team. That same season he broke a leg and had to wait another seven years before returning to League football, when he became top Football League goal-scorer in 1964/65 with thirty-six goals — still with Doncaster Rovers.

Celtic became the first British winners of the European Cup in 1967.

There was not a single away win in any of the thirty-five FA Cup and League matches played on 30 January 1937.

Sheffield United's home ground, Bramall Lane, was the site of a cricket test match between England and Australia in 1902.

In 1975 Wimbledon became the first non-League club to win an FA Cup tie at a Division I ground for fifty-five years when they beat Burnley at Turf Moor.

Maria Coluna, who won European Cup winners' medals for Benfica in the 1960s, also held the long-jump record in Mozambique.

A. Ingham of Queen's Park Rangers, playing full-back against Gillingham in a Division III (South) match on 31 January 1953, scored a goal with a kick from inside his own half of the field.

In 1938 East Fife became the only Scottish Division II side to win the Scottish FA Cup.

The 1911/12 season was the last when a goalkeeper was allowed to handle the ball outside his penalty area.

A Spurs-Huddersfield League match in 1952 provided one of the most controversial goals ever in the Football League. Eddie Bailey took a re-taken corner which hit the referee on the back, bounced off to Bailey who chipped it to Len Duquemin, allowing him to score the only goal of the match. Huddersfield protested that Bailey had played the ball a second time before it touched another player, so infringing Law 17, but the unsighted referee and the League let the goal stand.

Kick-off

February is a make or break month for football clubs — it is to football what Tattenham Corner is to the Derby. If you have survived a couple of rounds of the FA Cup, you start to set your sights on Wembley by February. In the same way, if you have not got into a challenging position in the League by February, you and everybody else know that it will take an extraordinary run to achieve championship success by the end of the season.

It is very important for a club, as well as for the individual player, that February does not run out without something to look forward to. If you get knocked out of the Cup, and you are not up with the leaders, the structure of the League means that (unless you have the unwelcome excitement of fighting relegation) it really is a matter of just holding on from then until the end of the season — and February to May can be a long time to keep up this sort of rearguard action.

It is a chilly month, and one that can be very cold for those clubs out of the Cup and way behind in the League!

Having beaten Gainsborough Trinity 4–1 in a second-round FA Cup tie at Turf Moor on 1 February 1913, Burnley signed their opponent's goalkeeper and two full-backs and played them in their next match against Sheffield United.

On 1 February 1930 Joe Bambrick scored six goals in Northern Ireland's 7–0 victory over Wales, the highest individual tally in a home international.

In 1885 Luton Town became the first professional Football League side south of Birmingham.

Paddy Moore, a member of the Irish World Cup team in 1934, was the first man to score four goals in a World Cup match, when the Republic of Ireland drew 4–4 with Belgium in one of the qualifying matches.

February

Two northern clubs achieved record wins on 2 February. In 1897 Bury established theirs with a 12-1 victory over Stockton in an FA Cup first-round replay, and two years earlier Sunderland beat Fairfield 11-1 at the same stage in the FA Cup competition.

As a result of the delicate political situation at the time, Northern Ireland played their 1972 European championship match against Spain in February at Boothferry Park, Hull City's home ground.

Southport's leading goal-scorer at the end of the 1955/56 season in Division III (North) was their amateur player George Bromilow, with twenty-two goals.

Dundee United won their first major title, the Scottish FA Cup, when they eventually beat Clyde after two replays.

On 3 February 1957 Real Madrid lost at home to Athletico Madrid 2-3, the last time they lost a home match until 7 March 1965. During that time they won 114 and drew eight league games until they were finally beaten 0-1, again by Athletico Madrid!

Grimsby Town were among the founder members of Division II and Division III (North) and (South).

Between the two World Wars the Scottish trainer William Bar trained twelve clubs: Kilmarnock, Third Lanark, Raith Rovers, Sheffield Wednesday, Huddersfield, Port Vale, Luton, Walsall, Coventry, Bristol Rovers, Swindon and Exeter.

Jimmy Adamson was offered the job of England team manager before Alf Ramsey in 1962.

Jason Dozzell was sixteen years, fifty-seven days old when he scored for Ipswich in their match against Coventry on 4 February 1984, making him the youngest player to score in Division I.

On 4 February 1888 the Welsh international Jack Doughty was considered good enough to kick a ball 'past the moon' — the 'moon' on that occasion being the England goalkeeper, William Moon.

In 1920 Jimmy MacMenemy was given a free transfer from Celtic to Partick Thistle, after playing 450 games for the Glasgow club. The following year he won a Scottish FA Cup winners' medal with Partick.

At the end of the 1914/15 season Oldham Athletic were runners-up in Division I, just one point behind the champions Everton.

5 February 1963 was an important date in the life of David Sadler. Not only was he seventeen that day, but he also left Maidstone United and a job as a bank clerk to join Manchester United.

On 5 February 1958 Matt Busby's assistant manager at Manchester United, Jimmy Murphy, had to miss their European quarter-final match against Red Star Belgrade, because he was on managerial duty himself for Wales.

Burnley began their sporting life as a rugby club, playing at Calder Vale with the name Burnley Rovers. This was in 1881. The following year they changed both their sport and their ground.

In 1967 Basle won the Swiss Cup by default when their opponents walked off the pitch.

6

Billy Wright's birthday. During his playing career he was capped thirteen times for England in matches against Scotland, a record among England players.

This date is also the anniversary of one of the saddest events in British football, the Munich air-crash of 1958. After drawing 3-3 in their European quarter-final tie in Belgrade, Manchester United were flying home from their match with Red Star. At Munich the plane refuelled, but on take-off it crashed, killing eight players (Roger Bryne, Tommy Taylor, Duncan Edwards, David Pegg, Geoffrey Bent, Eddie Coleman, Mark Jones and Liam Whelan), trainer Tom Currey, coach Bert Whalley, secretary Walter Crickmer and eight sporting journalists, including the former Manchester City and England goalkeeper, Frank Swift. Others travelling in the plane were seriously injured, among them players like Jackie Blanchflower and Johnny Berry.

On **7 February 1920 Bob Benyon was Welsh stand-off in their rugby union international against Scotland. The following week he was playing centre-forward as a professional footballer for Swansea Town in their match with Queen's Park Rangers.**

In the 1967/68 season Peterborough were relegated from the Football League after an incident involving illegal payments.

The Swedish team that reached the finals of the World Cup in 1958 were managed by Yorkshireman George Raynor.

'Now then, Sven, win this one and it's mushy peas all round!'

The matches between Hibernian and Raith Rovers, and East Fife and Stenhousemuir on 8 February 1956 were the first Scottish FA Cup ties to be played under floodlights.

In the 1955/56 season Accrington Stanley fielded a side of players who had all been born in Scotland.

Before joining Celtic in 1951 Jock Stein had two years in the Welsh League with Llanelli.

When Don Ford came on as substitute for Scotland in their 1973 match against Czechoslovakia, he could be described as a complete all-rounder. Not only was he an international footballer, he had been twelfth man in the Scottish cricket team, was a councillor in his native Linlithgow and ran his own business as a chartered accountant.

9 February 1963 was the worst day of the season for weather in both the English and Scottish Leagues. Fifty-seven games were postponed as a result of the snow and ice and in all only seven Football League games could be played, while the entire Scottish League programme was wiped out.

For their first twenty-one games in Division III (South) in 1950/51 Norwich City fielded an unchanged team.

In 1962 Michael Gliksten became chairman of Charlton Athletic at the age of twenty-three after being on the board for five years.

In 1969 Preben Arentoft of Denmark became the first overseas player to win a European competitor's medal with a British club while playing for Newcastle United.

10

Danny Blachflower's birthday. With a total of thirteen Northern Ireland caps against Scotland he holds a record among Irish players.

The creation of Stirling Albion Football club came about as the result of miscalculations by a Second World War German bomber. On its way home after a raid on the Clyde the aircraft dropped a number of bombs still on board over the quiet town of Stirling and the picturesque Forth Bank ground, home of King's Park Football Club, crumbled under the onslaught, so ending one football era and heralding another. As the war came to a close, a local consortium, led by a coal merchant, Tom Ferguson, came up with a plan to rebuild and relocate the club at Anfield Park, and in 1945 Stirling Albion was formed. In 1971 they were managed by Bob Shankly whose brother Bill was manager at that other Anfield (Liverpool).

11

The Hibernian player Joe Baker scored nine goals for his side in their match against Peebles Rovers on 11 February 1961.

The great Billy Meredith, who played forty-eight home international championship matches between 1895 and 1920, played for three Football League clubs: Manchester United, Manchester City and Northwich Victoria, which played in the League for just two seasons, 1882/83 and 1883/84.

Hector Castro, who scored in the first World Cup final in 1930, had only one arm.

The awarding of one point for a draw was introduced into the Football League for the tenth match of the first season in 1888/89.

The crowd of 48,110 that went to Villa Park in 1972 to watch Aston Villa play against Bournemouth in a League match was the highest ever to watch a Division II game in England.

During the Second World War Aldershot were fortunate in including many guest players in their side, among them Frank Swift, Tommy Lawton, Matt Busby, Denis Compton, Stan Cullis and Joe Mercer.

In the first season of the Football League, 1888/89, Preston became the first club to achieve the 'double'. Out of twenty-two games they won eighteen and drew the remaining four. They scored seventy-four goals and conceded only fifteen, and won the FA Cup without conceding a goal either.

In one 1938 FA Cup tie F. Bokas of Barnsley scored a goal with a throw.

On 13 February 1954 Raith Rovers set up a Scottish FA Cup record away from home when they scored a 10–1 victory over Coldstream.

Burnley were awarded a record four penalties in their Division II game against Grimsby Town on 13 February 1909. However, they also established two other records when they missed three of them and allowed the Grimsby goalkeeper, W. Scott, to set a record of his own by saving three. The one penalty that found its way into the net, added to a previous goal, gave Burnely a 2–0 victory.

Ted Croker, whose birthday is 13 February, became the first ex-professional footballer to become secretary of the Football Association. He played at full-back for Charlton Athletic during the 1940s and was a member of the FA Cup winning team in 1947.

February

(14)

Kevin Keegan's birthday. As a young player he was passed over by the Doncaster Schoolboy selection committee.

When Football League matches were suspended at the outbreak of the Second World War Middlesbrough had finished bottom of Division I in the previous season. However, they waited another eight seasons before finally being relegated. The story was less lucky for Blackpool, the League leaders that season. They never reached that pinnacle again, their best position being runners-up, eleven points behind the champions Manchester United in 1956.

Only once in the history of the Football League has the FA Cup final been contested by the League champions and their runners-up. This was in 1913 when Aston Villa beat Sunderland 1–0 to reverse their League placings.

(15)

Thirty-nine League and Cup games were postponed in England and Scotland due to the appalling weather on 15 February 1958.

Alec and David Herd became the only father and son to play in the same Football League match when they represented Stockport County in a Division III (North) game against Hartlepool.

In the 1976/77 season Hearts were relegated from the Scottish League for the first time since being one of its founder members in 1890.

In the history of the Football League the roll call of players has included Charlie Chaplin (Wolves), Bernard Shaw (Sheffield United), Bob Hope (West Brom), Winston Churchill (Chelsea), Trevor Howard (Bournemouth) and Baden Powell (Birmingham).

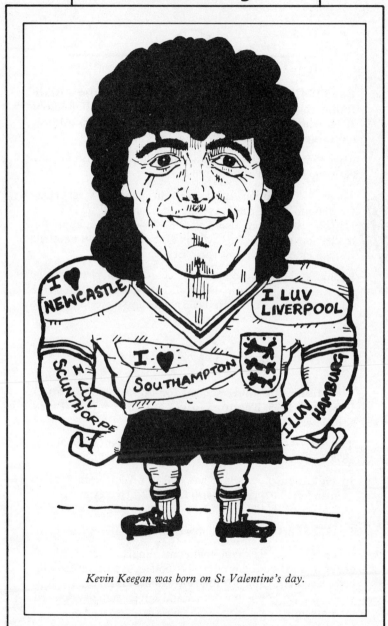

Kevin Keegan was born on St Valentine's day.

Cardiff City players Fred Keenor and Jimmy Blair found themselves on opposing sides on 16 February 1924, when Keenor captained Wales against Scotland, captained by Blair.

Mike Pinner of Pegasus won fifty-one England amateur caps between 1955 and 1963.

Thames Association, who used to play at West Ham Greyhound and Speedway stadium, competed in Division III (South) between 1930 and 1932. They did not apply for re-election after that, so becoming the only London Football League club to have lost their League status.

Bobby Collins played in a record twenty-two post-war seasons, with Celtic, Everton, Leeds, Bury, Morton and Oldham Athletic. He played 653 games and scored 163 goals.

The Hibbitt brothers scored for opposing sides on 17 February 1975, Ken for Wolves and his brother Terry for Newcastle.

The referee's whistle was first blown in a football match in 1878 between Notts Forest and Sheffield Norfolk.

In 1961 Denis Law scored six goals for Manchester City in an abandoned FA Cup tie with Luton. When they met for the replay Luton won!

In 1972 Spurs beat Wolves to win the first UEFA Cup final.

When George Eastham made his England international debut in 1963 he followed in the footsteps of his father who had played one game for England against the Netherlands in 1935, so making the only father and son team to have played for England.

On 18 February 1882 England beat Ireland 13–0, the highest score in a home international — Vaughan got five goals, A. Brown four, S. Brown two and Cursham and Bambridge one each.

Burnley had a run of thirty Division I games without a defeat in the 1920/21 season.

In 1959 Crystal Palace's Vic Rouse became the first Division IV player to win an international cap when he was picked to play for Wales against Northern Ireland.

Kubala and Di Stefano played international football for three different countries, but the lesser known Scottish player Jim Kennaway achieved the same feat by representing the USA, Canada and Scotland.

The former England international Bobby Benson died under tragic circumstances on 19 February 1916. After going to watch Arsenal play at Reading, he was persuaded to take the field with Arsenal in spite of not having played for a year. His exertions proved too much for him and he collapsed and died in the dressing-room after the game.

A record crowd of 33,042 (almost 6,000 over the ground's capacity) went to Reading's Elm Park on 19 February 1927 to watch their fifth round FA Cup tie with Brentford.

Gylmar, the goalkeeper, was the only member of the Brazilian side to play at Wembley in both 1956 and 1963.

In 1971 and 1972 Stoke City achieved the unenviable record of losing to the same opposition in successive FA Cup semi-finals and never reaching Wembley.

Peter Osgood's birthday. Chelsea discovered him after replying to a letter from a fond uncle in his home town of Windsor asking if his seventeen-year-old nephew could be given a trial.

O. Ohlsson of Gothenberg was the first man to score five goals in a European Cup tie when the Swedish side played Linfield in 1960.

Between 1927 and 1936 J.C. Burns, playing at left-half, made 263 appearances for Queen's Park Rangers, all of them as an amateur.

Nottingham Forest is the only Football League club not to have formed a limited company.

During the 1958 World Cup finals Wolves provided England with the complete half-back line: Clamp, Wright and Slater.

Alex Dawson, who started his professional career with Manchester United after the Munich tragedy, was born in Aberdeen on 21 February 1940. As a schoolboy international he captained England against Scotland. The Scottish captain, Joe Baker, had been born in Liverpool!

In 1931 Wigan became the first club to resign from the Football League, having their record wiped out. The following year Wigan Athletic was formed.

In 1966 Munoz of Real Madrid became the first man to both play in and manage European Cup winning sides.

When Rangers won the Scottish FA Cup in 1948 and 1949 W. Williamson made appearances once in both campaigns; he played in the two finals.

The first Football League game under floodlights was between Portsmouth and Newcastle United, played at Fratton Park on 22 February 1956.

In the 1922/23 season Southampton achieved the unusual record of winning, losing and drawing fourteen games; they also scored forty goals and conceded forty!

The 1962 Football League Cup final was between Norwich of Division II and Rochdale of Division IV, making it the first major English Cup final not to have involved a Division I club.

Alec Jackson became the first player to score a hat-trick against England when Scotland played England at Wembley in 1928.

In 1957 Stoke City's winger Neville Coleman scored seven goals in their Division II match against Lincoln City, a record by a winger in the Football League.

Eight Italian internationals were killed when the entire Torino side died in an air crash in 1949.

In 1966 the Mexican goalkeeper Antonio Carbajal played in his fifth World Cup final.

The crossbar was first used in a football match in 1875.

Leeds United became the first British winners of the European Fairs Cup in 1968.

The former West Ham player John Lyall was born on 24 February 1940 and in 1974 became only the club's fifth manager this century, the others being Syd King (1900–31), Charlie Paynter (1931–50), Ted Fenton (1950–61) and Ron Greenwood (1961–74).

Between 1958 and 1971 Standard Liège won six Belgian League titles, six European cups and reached the quarter-finals four times.

At the start of the 1972/73 season the shortest distance Plymouth Argyll had to travel for a Division III match was 118 miles to play Bristol Rovers.

Ferenc Puskas, the famous Hungarian footballer of the 1950s and 1960s, was nicknamed Ocsi, which means 'kid brother' in Hungarian.

During an Amateur Cup match between Highgate United and Enfield Town on 25 February 1967 Tommy Alden, one of the Highgate players, was struck by lightning.

At the end of the 1954/55 season Birmingham, Luton and Rotherham finished level in Division II with fifty-four points, but Birmingham and Luton were the clubs to be promoted; Rotherham's centre-half had missed a penalty against Port Vale.

Sandor Kosis of Barcelona was the first player to score four goals in a European Cup match against a British club in 1960 when he achieved this feat at the expense of Wolves.

In 1973 the New Zealand cricketer Vic Pollard declined to join his country's World Cup squad, in order to tour England with the New Zealand cricket team.

Pat Jennings became the first British player to take part in 1,000 first-class games when Arsenal played West Brom on 26 February 1983. He played in 695 Football League games, 95 internationals, 3 Under-23, 81 FA Cup, 65 League/Milk Cup, 55 European, 2 Charity Shield, 2 Texaco Cup and 2 Anglo-Italian Cup games.

Arthur Trevis, the West Bromwich Albion centre-half of the 1930s, had no fewer than seven christian names: Arthur, Griffith, Stanley, Sackville, Redvers, Trevor, Boscawen. His team mates opted to call him Bos for short.

Queen of the South Football Club was formed in 1919 as an amalgamation of Arrol-Johnson Football Club, Dumfries Football Club and K.O.S.B.

Nobby Stiles is married to Johnny Giles's sister.

England played their first match under Alf Ramsey on 27 February 1963, a European Nations Cup tie against France in Paris, which the French won 5–2 (the English goals coming from Smith and Tambling). It was a rough day for another newcomer to international football, a *Daily Mail* reporter covering his first international match. He was completing the fifth page of his report when the phone rang, a signal from his Fleet Street office to begin dictating. As he lifted the receiver his elbow shifted the typewriter and the completed pages blew away. The one page he did manage to grab started, 'In the seventy-second minute of the match...'

Blackpool's 'Jock' Dodds scored the fastest hat-trick in British football in two and half minutes against Tranmere Rovers on 28 February 1943.

Between 1927 and 1937 Walsall had ten different Football League managers: D. Ashworth, J. Torrance, J. Kerr, S. Scholey, J. Burchell, P. O'Rourke, G. Saunders, W. Slade, A.N. Wilson and T. Lowes.

Sunderland's goalkeeper James Thorpe died a few days after his team had played against Chelsea in February 1936. His death was due to diabetes, but the coroner's jury found that the illness had been accelerated by his rough handling as a goalkeeper.

The 1950 Swedish World Cup star Hans Jeppson scored thirteen goals in eleven matches when he was playing for Charlton in the same year.

A. Brown of Sheffield United played for England against Wales on 29 February 1904, when he was two months short of his nineteenth birthday. At centre-forward he was the youngest-ever international in that position.

The Irish League club Linfield play at Windsor Park, Northern Ireland's international venue.

The Swedish side that won the 1948 Olympic football competition included three brothers: Knut, Bertil and Gunner Nordhal.

The Arsenal goalkeeper Bob Wilson turned down the opportunity from Sir Matt Busby to join Manchester United when he was fifteen.

Charles Burgess Fry, who was capped for England against Ireland in 1901, also played right-back for Southampton in the 1900 Cup final. He was perhaps the greatest all-rounder of his day: at Oxford he had taken a first-class degree, played cricket and football for the university and had also held the world long-jump record. He later played cricket for Surrey, Sussex, Hampshire and England and also represented his country in athletics.

In February 1965 Stanley Matthews became the only outfield player to play in a League match past his fiftieth birthday, when Stoke beat Fulham 3–1.

Manchester United were the first English winners of the European Cup in 1968.

'He may not look much, but he's got a great body swerve.'

Kick-off

For years, 16 March was the closing date for football transfers. It is also my eldest son's birthday, so it is a date that carries a double significance for me.

I was transferred from Brentford to Fulham in 1953, and Duncan was born shortly afterwards. The deal involved a fee of five thousand pounds in addition to Jimmy Bowie as a trade — twenty thousand had been paid for him, so by my reckoning I was transferred for twenty-five thousand pounds, which in those days was a staggeringly high fee!

From a manager's point of view, this is the critical period for making any last-minute changes to the team if you are in with a chance of promotion, or are fighting off relegation. I did it one year when I was managing Coventry City, and we bought John Smith and George Kirby. On one particular Friday evening we had been leading the Third Division by nine points (it was eight at the end of the next day). But we then went for twelve matches without winning a game. We had lost a couple of good players through injury, and I took the plunge and made the replacements by buying the two extra players. Fortunately it paid off, and we managed to scramble back and came top of the Division by a tiny margin.

There is another memory milestone of mine in March, dating from an away match we played against Doncaster Rovers in 1959. Fulham won 6-1 and I scored five of the goals — the second highest away game goal-scoring record in League history. (The highest was Ted Drake's total of seven for Arsenal before the war at Villa Park.) Luck was with me that day. I only had seven shots at goal, five went in the net and the other two ended as good saves. Mind you, there were plenty of other matches when I missed the goal completely. I suppose I was just fortunate that the law of averages decided to even things out that one afternoon.

March

T. Ward was made manager of Exeter City at the beginning of March 1953 only to become manager of his old club Barnsley twenty-five days later. He was with Exeter for just seven days, after which Barnsley, who still held his registration as a player, recalled him to their ranks.

In the 1948/49 season Portsmouth became the first Football League club to become Division I champions after rising from Division III.

The Pegasus side that beat Bishop Auckland 2–1 to win the Amateur Cup final of 1951 contained Oxford and Cambridge varsity players, among them double blue Tony Dawson and England cricket captain D.B. Carr. Their coach was Vic Buckingham who managed English League clubs in the 1960s and 70s.

During a Division I game between West Ham and Manchester City on 2 March 1932 one of the West Ham full-backs, A. Chalkley, kicked a goal from inside his own half of the field.

Brian Godfrey became the first player from Scunthorpe United to play representative football when he was picked for the Welsh Under-23s against the Irish Under-23s in 1962.

An ex-Huddersfield and Bolton player, George Barlow, was given an unexpected bonus from the game when he won £150,000 on the Littlewood pools in 1961.

On 3 March 1928 R. Dix became the youngest goal-scorer in the Football League when at the age of fifteen years, 180 days he scored for Bristol Rovers in their Division III (South) game against Norwich City. He had made his League debut seven days earlier in a match against Charlton Athletic.

Field Marshal Viscount Montgomery of Alamein was once president of Portsmouth.

The Liverpool wingers Ian Callaghan and Peter Thompson were once described as 'Ramsey's flirtation and Shankly's love affair'. They were regarded as the best pair of wingers since 1945 and though winning twenty caps between them (Callaghan four, Thompson sixteen) they never played together for England.

When Jock Spelton joined Holt United from Mossend Celtic an unusual fee was involved — thirty sheets of corrugated iron which Mossend Celtic needed for a fence round their ground.

Manchester United once signed a player from Stockport County, Hugh McLenahan, for a fee of three freezers full of ice cream.

Paula O'Sullivan might have cause to be less than enthusiastic about Liverpool's FA Cup victory in 1965. She was christened soon afterwards and given the names of the winning side, so that her birth certificate read: Paula, St John, Lawrence, Lawler, Byrne, Strong, Yates, Stevenson, Callaghan, Hunt, Milne, Smith, Thompson, Shankley, Bennett, Paisley, O'Sullivan. Her father was a devoted Liverpool supporter, so much so that he ignored minor details like the correct spelling of the captain Yeats and the manager Shankly.

The first £500,000 pools payout came on 4 March 1972 when Cyril Grimes, a £20-a-week wages clerk, collected £512,683 from a 30p stake.

Kenny Dalglish was born in Glasgow on 4 March 1951.

Between 1927 and 1946 Arsenal had five doctors: James Paterson, Jimmy Marshall, George Little, Kevin O'Flanagan and Alec Cross.

Jimmy Seed, manager of Charlton Athletic, made a bid to buy Stanley Matthews from Stoke City in 1938. The deal was finalized with the Stoke manager Bob McGrory, but the board of directors would not agree to it. In the words of the Charlton chairman, Albert Gliksten, 'A good job we didn't buy Matthews, it would have been £13,000 down the drain.'

Thirty-three people died at Burnden Park on 5 March 1946 when thousands of spectators forced their way into the ground to watch an FA Cup quarter-final between Bolton and Stoke City. In the course of the surge to get into the match several barriers collapsed causing the tragic loss of life.

A team selected from London clubs played Barcelona in the first final of the European Fairs Cup on 5 March 1958. The first leg played at Stamford Bridge ended in a 2–2 draw, with English goals from Jimmy Greaves and Jim Langley. Barcelona won the cup however, after a 6–0 victory in the second leg.

Until the change to the present rule, teams used to change ends after each goal.

Kenny Dalglish was born on 4 March 1951.

March

Accrington Stanley resigned from the Football League on 6 March 1962.

In the 1964/65 season Northampton Town became the first team to reach Division I after being promoted from Division IV and up through Divisions III and II.

The Scottish Cup was withheld in 1909 because the two matches between Celtic and Rangers had ended in draws, which caused a riot among their spectators.

The Belgian international J. Jurion, who played for his country forty-nine times, wore glasses during his entire career.

'That's the last time I try heading a ball!'

When **Middlesbrough beat Sheffield United 1-0 on 7 March 1903 it proved to be their last away win in the Football League for almost two years. Only the timely signing of A. Common in February 1905 spared them from relegation. In their match against Sheffield United later in the month Common scored the only goal of the match with a penalty and gave them their first away win since their 1903 meeting with United.**

Brechin, with a population of around 6,000, claims the smallest number of inhabitants supporting a League club in Great Britain.

After joining Swansea in 1919 left-back Wilf Milne had to wait until his 501st appearance before scoring his first goal.

1967 was the first time that the League Cup winners qualified for Europe, but it was Queen's Park Rangers plight that they had to be a Division I club as well.

Four penalties were awarded within five minutes during a Division III (North) match betwen Crewe and Bradford on 8 March 1924.

Vic Buckingham, a famous English Football League manager of the late 1960s and early 70s, managed both Ajax and Barcelona during his career.

1927 was a memorable year for Welsh football. Cardiff took the FA Cup out of England for the only occasion in its history, Aberdare lost their league status and Swansea beat Real Madrid 3-0.

A former York City goalkeeper, George Thompson, had a particular reason for going to watch one Division III (North) game between his old club and Scunthorpe — on this occasion his sons were rival goalkeepers.

March

9

9 March 1966 is remembered as the night George Best dazzled Benfica's Stadium of Light in Manchester United's second-leg European Cup quarter-final match against the Portuguese side. United had won the first leg at Old Trafford 3–2 and took the second 5–1. Best scored twice in the opening twelve minutes and ran rings round the Benfican defence whenever he had the ball. He was not fully fit after an injury when the first leg of the European Cup semi-final was played away against Partizan Belgrade and went straight into hospital for a cartilage operation after the game. United lost that tie 1–2 and Best was out of action for the rest of the season. Two years later, though, they finally clinched the European Cup.

During the Scottish League Division I match between Celtic and Airdrie on 10 March 1965 Bertie Auld, playing at wing-forward for Celtic, scored five goals including two penalties.

Malcolm Macdonald started his football career with the Southern League club Tonbridge before joining Fulham in 1968 as a full-back.

Workington had more directors in 1966 (thirteen) than full-time players. At the end of the season they finished bottom of Division III.

Reading's Jack Lewis scored fifteen goals in the 1951/52 season playing at wing-half, more than any player other than a forward that season.

11 March is the earliest date on which an FA Cup final has been played. On 11 March 1876 The Wanderers beat the Old Etonians 3–0.

When Andy Beattie was appointed manager of Notts County in March 1967 he became the first person to have managed eight football clubs, the others being Barrow, Stockport County, Huddersfield, Carlisle, Notts Forest, Plymouth and Wolves.

Arsenal started life in 1884 as Dial Square Football Club.

F. Binder became the first man to score 1,000 goals in a Football League career when he achieved this tally in 1950.

When England beat West Germany 2–0 on 12 March 1975 it was the 100th international played at Wembley Stadium. The first international there had been a match between England and Scotland on 12 April 1924 that ended in a 1–1 draw.

In 1962 Herbert Lister became the first man to score six goals in a Division IV match when Oldham Athletic beat Southport 11–0.

In 1979 Brian Talbot became the first player to win successive FA Cup winners' medals with different clubs: Ipswich in 1978 and Arsenal in 1979.

Chelsea, the 1955 Football League champions, did not enter the first European Cup and were replaced by Guardia Warsaw. Hibernian carried the British flag however, and won through to the semi-finals.

Bob Crompton broke Steve Bloomer's record number of England caps on 13 March 1911 when he won his twenty-fourth in a match against Wales. (Today's record is held by Bobby Moore with 108!)

In 1949 Carlisle United's player-manager Ivor Broadis transferred himself to Sunderland.

The non-League Welsh club Bangor City took the Italian Division I club Roma to two replays before finally losing in the 1962/63 European Cup-winners' Cup.

The USSR international V. Brobrov played in the 1952 Olympic ice hockey championships.

The Irish League was formed on 14 March 1890.

Clapton Orient's ground at Lea Bridge was banned for a while in the 1930/31 season because it did not meet with official standards, so they used Wembley Stadium for two of their League games against Brentford and Southend.

Tom Hutchinson of Manchester City had the unenviable distinction of scoring for both sides in the 1981 FA Cup final against Spurs which ended in a 1–1 draw! In doing this he emulated Bert Turner's feat in the 1947 Cup final when he scored for both sides in Charlton's 1–4 defeat by Derby County. In 1981 Spurs went on to win the replay and took the Cup.

Willie Maley managed Celtic for fifty years before the Second World War.

In a match between the Argentinian sides Independiente and Gimnasia on 15 March 1973 one of the Independiente players, Maglioni, scored a hat-trick in one minute fifty seconds.

F. Osborne, who played for Fulham, was capped to play for England in the 1923 game against Northern Ireland, the first South African-born player to represent England in an international.

Everton was one of the founder members of the Football League in 1888 and has had only four seasons out of Division I: 1930/31, 1951/52, 1952/53 and 1953/54.

Neil McBain was the oldest player to make an appearance in a Football League match: he played in goal for New Brighton against Hartlepool aged fifty-two years four months.

Neil McBain was the oldest player to make an appearance in a Football League match.

Four goalkeepers were used in the England-Wales international at Wrexham on 16 March 1908. The England goalkeeper throughout was Bailey of Leicester Fosse, but the Welsh first choice, Leigh Roose, was injured in the first half and was replaced by the full-back Morris. In the second half England allowed the Welsh to bring on Davies of Bolton in place of Morris.

The first FA Cup final was played at the Kensington Oval on 16 March 1872; receipts at the gate amounted to £100!

Robert Stuart of Middlesbrough scored five own goals during the 1934/35 seaon.

When Danny Blanchflower started his RAF aircrew training he shared a hut with Richard Burton.

The last match between the English and Scottish Leagues was played on 17 March 1976.

Northern Ireland's international Bertie Peacock played 350 times for Glasgow Celtic between 1949 and 1960.

By spring 1985 only four current Division II clubs had never played in Division I: Oxford, Shrewsbury, Barnsley and Wimbledon. Oxford put this right by winning promotion at the end of the season.

Peter Braine, who was capped for Belgium during the 1920s also fenced for his country in the Olympic Games and his brother Ray captained Europe against England in 1938 to commemorate the England team's seventy-fifth anniversary.

When Chris Woods played in goal for Notts Forest in their League Cup final victory on 18 March 1978 he became the first man to play in a Wembley final before making his League debut.

In 1919 Leeds City were expelled from Division II after making illegal payments. Their place was taken by Port Vale who in 1968 were themselves expelled for the same reason, though they were soon readmitted.

Neil Franklin, England's centre-half just after the Second World War, created a sensation at the time by joining the Santa Fe club in Bogota.

The first Italian Under-23 team was managed by Piola who had played in the 1934 and 1938 World Cup winning teams.

Montrose have only ever provided two internationals, Gordon Brown at right-back and Alex Keiller at inside-left. They both played for Scotland against Northern Ireland on 19 March 1892.

In 1920 Belgium became the last host nation to win the Olympic football tournament in one of the most controversial incidents in Olympic history. In the final they played Czechoslovakia who, having had a player sent off, failed to get satisfaction from the English referee John Lewis, walked off the pitch and were disqualified. The title was awarded to Belgium by default.

Billy Bly joined Hull City as a goalkeeper in 1938 and twenty-two years, fourteen fractures and over 400 appearances later he retired.

At twenty-one Alan Ball was the youngest member of England's 1966 World Cup winning team.

When **Johnny Lambie played for Scotland in their match against Ireland on 20 March 1886 he was seventeen years 92 days old, the youngest player ever to appear for Scotland.**

When Sunderland was founded in 1879 they were known as Sunderland and District Teachers Amateur Football Club for their first two years.

Spurs made their European debut in 1962 when they lost 2–4 to the Polish League side Gornick in the European Cup. When it came to playing the home leg they won 8–1.

The first FA Cup match played under floodlights was a tie between Kidderminster Harriers and Brierley Hill Alliance in 1955.

The first goal scored in a Scottish FA Cup final came from Queen's Park W. McKinnon in their 2–0 victory over Clydesdale on 21 March 1874.

Between 1966 and 1967 Bristol City played fifty-two consecutive League and FA Cup games without using a substitute.

Dr V.E. Milne of Aston Villa became the first amateur to play in an FA Cup final in the 1924 match at Wembley.

The Austrian player Gerhardt Hanappi was voted Austrian footballer of the year every year between 1954 and 1960.

The referee's final whistle can never have been so important as at the end of the FA Cup semi-final game between Sheffield Wednesday and Huddersfield Town on 22 March 1930. As the whistle was blown a shot from Wednesday's Jack Allen was entering the net, but the referee refused to allow the goal because the ball had not crossed the line when the whistle was blown, and Huddersfield won 2-1. Jack Allen received some compensation two years later when Newcastle played in the final and he scored two goals to give them victory.

Between 1946/47 and 1955 Harold Bell made a record 401 appearances for Tranmere Rovers in Division III (North).

One of the most talented players in Danish football was Knud Lundberg who was in the 1948 Olympic side as well as being a doctor, a politician, a journalist and a novelist.

By 23 March 1970 Leeds United were on the brink of an amazing treble: they were in the semi-final of the European Cup, were leading the championship table and were facing Manchester United in an FA Cup semi-final replay. However, they ended up losing everything, playing eight fixtures in twenty-two days. They lost 1-3 on aggregate to Celtic in the European Cup, finished runners-up to Everton in the League by nine points and after reaching the FA Cup final lost to Chelsea in a replay.

In 1974 Scotland won their first World Cup match by beating Zaïre 2-0. They had previously drawn one and lost four games.

Leeds, the last winners of the European Fairs Cup in 1971, were knocked out of the first round of the UEFA Cup in 1972 when they lost the home leg 0-4 to Lierse.

England played their first international, against Romania, on 24 March 1939, winning 2–0.

Preston's left-half Jimmy Milne missed the 1938 FA Cup final with a broken collar bone. His son Gordon missed the 1965 final for Liverpool as a result of injury as well.

According to one Cambridge United supporter, 'League football in Cambridge is like having bingo in the Albert Hall.'

Glasgow Rangers provided the entire Scottish half-back line for the 1928 international against Northern Ireland: Muirhead, Meiklejohn (captain) and Craig.

Harold McNeil and his brother Moses played together on 25 March 1876 when Scotland faced Wales.

Before the 1886/87 season Scottish clubs were allowed to compete in the FA cup. Queen's Park twice reached the final, in 1884 and 1885, losing on both occasions to Blackburn Rovers. Five other Scottish clubs competed during this period as well: Hearts, Partick Thistle, Glasgow Rangers, Renton and Cowlairs.

North Korea, one of the success stories of the 1966 World Cup series, was eliminated from the competition in 1970 for refusing to play against Israel on political grounds.

Elton John is the nephew of Roy Dwight who scored in the 1959 FA Cup final for Nottingham Forest.

'League football in Cambridge is like having bingo in the Albert Hall.'

On 26 March 1921 Burnley were beaten 0–3 away by Manchester City, ending a run of thirty victories that had begun on 4 September 1920, the longest ever in a single season in the Football League. Burnley went on to win the Cup that season and Manchester City were the beaten finalists.

Herbert Chapman, who managed both Arsenal and Huddersfield Town to Division I championship hat-tricks, had his first managerial success in 1908/09 with Northampton.

Kevin Howley, who refereed the FA Cup Final in 1960, was just thirty-five at the time, the youngest man ever to be picked for the match.

When Alf Ramsey became England's manager, Jackie Milburn succeeded him at Ipswich Town.

When Hamilton Academicals beat Rangers 3–1 on 27 March 1929 they brought to an end a run of thirty-eight consecutive Scottish League Division I wins that had started almost a year earlier on 17 March 1928.

When William Wright joined Blackpool from a junior club in 1951 the transfer fee consisted of a set of tangerine shirts.

Persistence rewarded Yugoslavia in the 1960 Olympics when they beat Denmark in the final 3–1. They had previously come runners-up in 1948, 1952 and 1956.

Andy Beattie was appointed team manager for Scotland in 1954, but he resigned, disillusioned, during the World Cup finals that year after Scotland had lost 0–1 to Austria and 0–7 to Uruguay. All the same he was re-appointed five years later.

The FA Cup mid-week attendance record was established on 28 March 1946 when a crowd of 80,407 went to Maine Road to watch a semi-final replay between Derby County and Birmingham City.

Coventry City Football Club was founded in 1883 and until 1895 was known as Singers Football Club, after workers at the Singer Cycle factory who had been instrumental in its foundation.

In the 1972 UEFA Cup Wolves beat Den Haag 7–1 on aggregate, including three own goals scored in the away leg.

The Scottish Cup final has been held outside Glasgow on only one occasion; that was in 1896 when it was staged at St Bernard's Ground, Logie Green, where Hearts beat Hibs 3–1.

When Billy Meredith played for Manchester City against Newcastle United in an FA Cup semi-final on 29 March 1924, at forty-nine and eight months he became the oldest player ever to appear in the FA Cup competition proper. He was also the oldest player to play in a home international, when at almost forty-six, he played for Wales against England on 15 March 1920.

In 1931 Newcastle and Portsmouth played in a Division I match that resulted in a 0-0 draw without a single corner kick in the entire game.

After winning the 1952 FA Cup final Newcastle United went on a tour of South Africa, taking the cup with them. They played sixteen games, won fifteen and scored a total of seventy-three goals.

On 30 March 1946 Stockport County and Doncaster Rovers played a Northern Section Cup tie that lasted 205 minutes. Many spectators went home for tea and returned to find that the weary players had still not managed to kick a winning goal. The game finally ended with a 4–4 draw.

In 1967 65,000 people watched the Everton-Liverpool local derby at Goodison Park and a further 40,000 watched the game on closed-circuit television in Stanley Road.

Ireland first won the home international championship in 1912 having beaten Wales 2–1, England 3–0, and drawing 1–1 with Scotland.

The 1953 Amateur Cup final between Pegasus and Harwich attracted a crowd of 100,000.

The first representative match was played on 31 March 1866 when London beat Sheffield 2–0 at Battersea Park.

Scotland beat England 5–1 at Wembley on 31 March 1928, which was hailed as their most famous victory. According to the football commentator, Ivor Sharp, 'England were not merely beaten, they were bewildered — run to standstill.' In fact England managed just six shots during the whole match. Alec Jackson scored a hat-trick for Scotland and Alex James got the other two goals.

For a time Chesterfield displayed their patriotism by wearing Union Jack shirts.

The only occasion when players were numbered from 1 to 22 in an FA Cup final was in the 1933 game between Everton and Manchester City; this was the first year in which numbers were worn in the final.

Kick-off

As a player, I found April to be the month of hard grounds and an equally hard Easter programme. April showers may come readily to mind, but the warm spring breezes that dry out the ground are not easily forgotten by Football League players who have no skin on either hip bone by the end of the month.

Easter generally comes towards the end of April, too, just as the ground has started to go hard and rough. We used to play three fixtures: Good Friday, Easter Saturday and the Bank Holiday Monday. In recent years these have been staggered, but when that was the case there was barely time to grow a scab over a fresh graze before it was knocked off again; it must have been even more painful for rugby players!

With six points at stake in the space of four days at a critical time in the football year, there couldn't be any allowance for scrapes and bruises; and by the Easter Monday game I think most of us felt the match was a matter of physical endurance rather than of football skills!

'That's the new target man.'

April

When Wales beat Hungary 2-1 in Budapest on 1 April 1975 it was Hungary's first home defeat for thirty years. It was also the first time that a British team had won in Hungary since 1909, when between June 1908 and May 1909 England beat Hungary in Budapest on three occasions with wins of 7-0, 4-2 and 8-2, seven of which were scored by the great Vivian Woodward.

Scotland met England at Crystal Palace on 1 April 1903 wearing Lord Rosebery's racing colours of primrose and white hoops.

Nil Middleboe, who played for Denmark in the 1908, 1912 and 1920 Olympics, also played for Chelsea in the League.

The record attendance for a Division I match stands at 83,320 when Manchester United met Arsenal at Maine Road after the Second World War (Old Trafford was unsuitable at the time as a result of bomb damage).

Duncan Edwards became England's youngest international on 2 April 1955 at the age of eighteen years 183 days. Just two months earlier he scored the first hat-trick in an Under-23 international.

Manchester United's Enoch West was given a life suspension that lasted thirty years after being found responsible (with others) for fixing the Manchester United-Liverpool match of 2 April 1915. His suspension was lifted in 1945 when he was sixty-two!

On 2 April 1977 Coventry City ended a succession of eight away fixtures in Division I that had begun on 29 January of that year.

Helenio Herrera, manager of Inter Milan's 1964/65 European Cup winning team, was the prime instigator of the 'sweeper', an extra defender whose job it was to shuttle from one side of the pitch to the other, to cut off any move that had penetrated the man-to-man marking of the back four.

The Division I game between Middlesbrough and Oldham Athletic on 3 April 1915 had to be abandoned after fifty-give minutes when Oldham's left-back W. Cook refused to leave the field when ordered off by the referee. At that stage Middlesbrough were leading 4–1 and the Football League decided that the result should stand at that. Cook was suspended for twelve months and Oldham missed the League championship by two points that season.

During the 1960/61 season Burnley were fined £1,000 for fielding ten reserves in a Division I game against Chelsea.

Stan Cullis had one of football's quickest rises to fame. He captained Wolves at eighteen; played for England against Romania when he was twenty-one and was manager of Wolves at thirty-two.

The average age of the Port Vale team that played Bradford City on 4 April 1966 was less than eighteen.

Since joining the Football League in 1885 Queen's Park Rangers have had eighteen different grounds and four changes of colours.

The original World Cup Jules Rimet trophy was designed by a French sculptor, Abel Lafleur. It was made of solid gold, weighed around nine pounds and stood about a foot high.

Somerset Park is not the name of the home ground of an English West Country club, but of the Scottish side, Ayr United.

Ron Haider of Hendon made his sixty-fifth amateur international appearance when he played for England against Scotland on 5 April 1974.

In addition to the terrible disaster of 1971, Ibrox Park in Glasgow was the scene of another tragedy on 5 April 1902, when part of a temporary wooden stand collapsed during an England-Scotland match and twenty-five people were killed.

I. Netto, who scored an own goal when captaining the USSR in the first European Nations Cup final, wrote an autobiography entitled *This Is Football*.

Johnny Haynes managed Fulham for seventeen days after Bobby Robson was sacked.

When Gillingham were beaten 2–3 at home by Barrow on 6 April 1963 it was to be their last defeat at Priestfield Stadium until they lost 0–1 to Exeter City, just over two years later on 10 April 1965. This established a record run in both FA and Football League cup home games and included forty-eight Football League games as well.

In 1935 Arsenal's Ted Drake scored seven goals against Aston Villa at Villa Park, from just eight shots — a feat achieved only once before, by Jimmy Ross of Preston in 1888.

At the start of the 1971/72 season Hull City had two international managers on their payroll, Tommy Docherty (Scotland) and Terry Neill (Northern Ireland).

Only one European Cup final has ever gone to a replay, when Bayern Munich finally beat Atletico Madrid 4-0, following a 1-1 draw, in 1974.

Alan Rough made his first appearance in goal for Scotland on 7 April 1976 in a match against Switzerland at Hampden Park. Fifty-one appearances later he played his last international, when Scotland played the USSR in Spain in 1982 during the World Cup finals.

In 1916 Hartlepool's ground was destroyed in a Zeppelin raid. They began taking legal action against the German government for compensation but the proceedings failed to gain any funds for the club.

When FC Magdeburg beat AC Milan in the final of the European Cup-winners' Cup in 1974 they became the first East German club to win a major European competition.

Preston and Burnley, both founder members of the Football League, have never met in the FA Cup.

On 8 April 1933 Reading lost at home to Brentford 1–3. They did not lose again in Football League home matches until being beaten by Queen's Park Rangers 1–2 on 15 January 1936. During their winning run they played fifty-five consecutive home League games without defeat.

In 1908 the Football Association set up a charity shield for an annual match between two teams selected by the Association with the proceeds to go to charity. The first final was played at Stamford Bridge in 1909 when the League champions Manchester United beat the Southern League champions Queen's Park Rangers 4–0, after a 1–1 draw.

The Rangers manager between 1920 and 1954, Willie Struth, won eighteen Scottish League championships, ten Scottish Cups and three League Cups.

Gillingham's run of fifty-two unbeaten home matches came to an end on 9 April 1965, after two years in which they established a record that wasn't beaten until Liverpool's succession of eighty-five home matches between January 1978 and January 1981.

Jimmy Dickinson played the last of his 764 League games for Portsmouth in April 1965. During his nineteen seasons at Fratton Park he had played in every League match in seven seasons, including all forty-six in Division III.

In 1964 seven players from Real Zaragoza represented Spain in an international.

Wales won the home championships in 1933, 1934 and 1937 and were undefeated from 1932 to 1934.

Jack Charlton made his England debut in the match against Scotland on 10 April 1965; his brother Bobby was playing in his fifty-eighth international in the same game.

The England outside-left L. Page was first tried at centre-forward for Burnley on 10 April 1926. The change in position proved to be a success: Page scored a double hat-trick that afternoon against Birmingham City.

Bob Hatton, who joined Wolves as an apprentice in 1964, then joined another seven clubs for which transfer fees were paid: Bolton in 1967 for £30,000; Northampton in 1968 for £30,000; Carlisle in 1969 for £15,000; Birmingham in 1971 for £75,000; Blackpool in 1975 for £50,000; Luton in 1978 for £50,000; and Sheffield United in 1980 for £50,000. In 1982 he joined Cardiff City on a free transfer.

During an Under-14 match on 11 April 1976 Midas Football Club beat Courage Colts 59–1. Courage scored first, but then Midas got into their stride; their top scorer being Kevin Graham with seventeen goals.

On the day that Billy Wright was selected to play his 100th international for England, 11 April 1959, his wife Joy, one of the Beverley sisters, gave birth to their first child.

The USSR won their first major European football trophy in 1975 when Dynamo Kiev beat Ferencvaros in the final of the European Cup-winners' Cup. In the same year the Soviet player Oleg Blockin was awarded the title of European footballer of the year.

Due to a dispute over the payment of expenses by South American countries, football was omitted from the 1932 Olympic Games.

Bobby Moore's birthday. In addition to holding the record number of 108 England caps, he also has the unique distinction of collecting the FA Cup, the European Cup-winners' Cup and the World Cup — all at Wembley.

Today is also the birthday of the Peruvian player Hector Chumpital, who between 1963 and 1981 played for his country 145 times.

In 1928 Newcastle United fielded ten Scottish-born players in a Division I match against Leeds. Only the centre-half, Wood, was born outside Scotland.

E. Streltson was banished from the USSR 1958 World Cup team to serve a twelve-year prison sentence. In 1967 he returned to become Russian footballer of the year.

Bobby Moore, holder of a record 108 England caps, celebrates his birthday on 12 April.

Joe Payne established his Football League goal-scoring record on 13 April 1936 when he kicked ten goals for Luton Town against Bristol Rovers in their Division III (South) match.

In 1936 Blackburn Rovers used five goalkeepers (Binns, Hughes, Barrow, Hammill and Pratt) in eight consecutive matches.

The Welsh international Billy Meredith played 670 Football League games and forty-eight internationals between 1895 and 1924, from which his average earnings amounted to four pounds fifteen shillings (£4.75) a week.

In the 1958/59 season Port Vale became the first champions of Division IV.

On 14 April 1900 Manchester United's goalkeeper, C. Williams, scored directly with a goal kick in a match against Sunderland. His opposite number, Ned Doig, managed to touch the ball on its way into the net, but failed to make the save!

When Carlisle United joined the Football League in 1928 they displaced Durham City, so preventing the possibility of a local derby.

In 1978 WAC Austria reached the final of the European Cup-winners' Cup after winning two ties on penalties and one on the away goals rule.

In the 1922/23 season Charlton Athletic knocked three Division I clubs out of the FA Cup.

The Scottish forward line picked to play England on 15 April 1950 were all called William: William Waddell, William Moir, William Bauld, William Steel and William Liddell.

On 15 April 1961 the third choice Scottish goalkeeper, Frank Haffy, had the misfortune to let in nine England goals during his only international appearance. England won at Wembley that afternoon 9–3.

The first substitute in an international took to the field during a Wales–Scotland match on 15 April 1889, when the Welsh player S. Gilliam was injured just after kick-off and was replaced by Pugh.

On 15 April 1916 Celtic played two League matches. In the afternoon they beat Raith Rovers 6–0 and in the evening they were victors in a 3–1 win over Motherwell.

On 16 April 1975 Malcolm Macdonald scored five goals for England in a match against Cyprus at Wembley, the only occasion that he scored for England in fourteen international appearances.

In the 1898/99 season Division II Darwin suffered three 0–10 defeats in away matches against Manchester City, Walsall and Loughborough Town.

Only Tommy Lawton remained in the England team that had played the last international before the Second World War against Romania when the first post-war side was chosen to play Northern Ireland.

Sheffield, formed in 1857, achieved only one major honour in their history, the 1904 Amateur Cup.

The Football League was formed on 17 April 1888 at the Royal Hotel, Piccadilly, Manchester. The original twelve members were Accrington, Aston Villa, Blackburn Rovers, Bolton Wanderers, Burnley, Derby County, Everton, Notts County, Preston North End, Stoke City, West Bromwich Albion and Wolverhampton.

At half-time during a friendly match between Stirling Albion and the Austrian club Admira on 17 April 1954, the Stirling chairman invited Dale Evans, Roy Rogers and Trigger to give a display.

The first pair of twins to score in the same Football League match were the Stephens (Alfred and William), who got the winning goals when Swindon beat Exeter 2–0 in a Division III (South) match in 1946.

During a Scottish League Division II game on 18 April 1936 J. Calder scored eight goals for Morton against Raith Rovers.

The Dutch player Bobby Rensenbrink scored the 1,000th World Cup final goal during the 1978 competition.

The French player Raymond Kupa featured in a unique tale of two cities during the European Cup finals of the late 1950s. In 1956 he played for Rheims in the first European Cup final against Real Madrid, which the Spanish side won 4–3. Shortly afterwards he joined Real Madrid for £50,000 and played in their next three European Cup final winning teams, including the one that beat Rheims 2–0 in 1959.

In 1906 Liverpool became the first club to top Division II and Division I in successive seasons.

On Good Friday 1957 (19 April) Chelsea became the first club to fly home from one match in order to play another the following day. After playing against Newcastle, they caught a plane, so that they would be able to face Everton at Stamford Bridge on Easter Saturday.

West Indian cricketer Viv Richards played for Antigua in the qualifying round of the 1978 World Cup.

In the 1945/46 season Aldershot's Harry Brooks scored five goals in successive FA Cup matches.

In 1971 the reigning Amateur Cup holders Skelmersdale United were fined £1,500 and had their chairman suspended for making illegal payments.

The last Amateur Cup final, the seventy-first, was played on 20 April 1974 when Bishop's Stortford beat Ilford 4-1.

An Act passed in 1314 prescribed imprisonment for anyone caught playing football in London. The popularity of the game was seen as a serious threat to national security, with the nation's bowmen playing football instead of archery practice.

Walter Winterbottom was the first England manager in a World Cup final, in 1958 in Stockholm. The Spurs manager, Bill Nicholson, was his assistant.

At the start of the 1984/85 season Notts County had played 3,385 Football League games.

(21)

Arthur Rowley, holder of the record for number of goals scored in Football League matches, was born on 21 April 1926. Between 1946 and April 1965 he scored 434 goals in the League as well as thirty-two in the FA Cup and one for England 'B'.

There are only six clubs in the Football League that have played all the other ninety-one: Barnsley, Bury, Grimsby, Lincoln, Northampton and Portsmouth.

In 1958 Nils Leidholm of Sweden and AC Milan won runners-up medals in both the World Cup and European Cup.

In 1936 Aston Villa and Blackburn Rovers were both relegated to Division II for the first time in their history.

(22)

E. Winstanley, playing at half-back for Barnsley, scored a hat-trick against Watford in a Division III match on 22 April 1969, equalling the record for a player in that position in a single game.

At the end of the 1979/80 season Leicester City won their sixth Division II title to equal Manchester City's record.

Since 1946 only one club has scored nine goals on three separate occasions in the FA Cup: Southend.

Russian teams took some heavy beatings in their early days. A combined Oxford and Cambridge side, the first British team to tour Russia, beat the national side 11–0 in 1911. The following year they were beaten 0–17 by Germany in the Stockholm Olympics.

April 1949 was a barren month for Southampton. Eight points clear at the top of Division II early in the month, they were subsequently overtaken by both West Brom and Fulham and had to wait a further seventeen years before gaining promotion to Division I.

The first Alliance Premier League in the 1979/80 season was won by Altringham.

In 1930 Everton became the last of the original twelve Division I clubs to be relegated.

R.E. Foster, who played for Oxford University and the Corinthians at football and for Oxford and Worcestershire at cricket, is the only man to have captained England at the two sports.

The closest finish to decide the Scottish Division I championship took place on 24 April 1965. It was the last day of the season and Hearts had a two-point lead at the top of the division over Kilmarnock and a slightly better goal average. They played each other that afternoon at Tynecastle Park (Hearts' home ground) and Kilmarnock won 2–0, taking the title by 0.04 of a goal.

When Jimmy Greaves was sent off in a European Cup-winners' Cup semi-final against OFK Belgrade on 24 April 1963, he was the first Spurs player to be sent off since Cecil Poynton thirty-five years earlier.

During the World Cup match between Poland and Argentina in 1978 the Polish captain Deyna had the bad luck to miss a penalty. This was all the more unfortunate since the game also marked his hundredth appearance for his country.

On **25 April 1970** England and Scotland ended an international match with a 0-0 score, the first time in their games against each other that this had happened.

While playing for Bradford Park Avenue against Tranmere on 25 April 1964, Jim Fryatt scored what is claimed to be the fastest Football League goal: four seconds. The referee, R.J. Simon, confirmed this on his stopwatch.

Manchester City was the first club to be relegated with a positive goal difference, at the end of the 1980/81 season.

European Cup finals probably provide mixed memories for Jimmy Rimmer. Having sat on the substitute's bench for Manchester United in the 1968 European Cup final, he fared slightly better in 1982 by lasting eight minutes on the pitch before being replaced by Nigel Spink.

The ball burst during the FA Cup final on **27 April 1946.** The referee, E.D. Smith, claimed that there was a one-in-a-million chance of it happening. Ironically exactly the same thing happened at the FA Cup final the following year!

April 1897 was a good month for Aston Villa, the year they became only the second club to achieve the double. On 10 April they beat Everton 3-2 in the FA Cup final, on the 17th they played their first match at Villa Park, beating Blackburn 3-0, on the 19th they crushed Wolves 5-0 and on 26 April they clinched the double at Preston with a 1-0 victory, so winning the title by eleven clear points from Sheffield United.

At twenty-four David Nish of Leicester City became the youngest man to captain a team at a Wembley Cup final when his side lost 0-1 to Manchester City on 26 April 1969.

Denis Law scored his last goal in first-class football
on 27 April 1974 at Old Trafford when he was playing
for Manchester City. Scoring in the eighty-fifth
minute of the match, he sent his old club Manchester
United into Division II.

There was a record attendance at Football League matches
during the 1948/49 season with 41,274,424 spectators.

Rising from his hospital bed after being immobilized for four
days with a knee injury, Manchester City's Colin Bell headed
for a hearty breakfast before going for a brisk three-mile walk
to get the muscles moving again and blow the cobwebs away.
Then a few hours later he skippered his team in their local
derby against Manchester United and scored a vital goal.

In the 1923/24 season Chesterfield's goalkeeper, A. Birch,
scored five goals, all penalties, and set a record for goals
scored by a goalkeeper in a single season.

The first FA Cup final, played at Wembley Stadium on
28 April 1923, was watched by an estimated
150,000–200,000 fans, the largest crowd ever to attend a
British football match. Kick-off was delayed by forty
minutes while mounted police, including PC George
Scorey on his famous white horse Billy, formed a
barrier that flanked the touchlines for the entire
games. Two minutes after the start Bolton's David
Jack became the first scorer in a Wembley FA Cup
final. Joe Smith, who later managed Blackpool when
they won the Cup in 1953, scored a second goal to give
Bolton a 2–0 victory over West Ham.

*The strain of waiting in goal for the final whistle of the FA Cup
final proved too much for the great Frank Swift on 28 April
1934. Listening to the photographers snapping away behind him
and musing on how difficult the cup was going to be to clean, the
pressure got to him and when the whistle finally blew, he fainted.*

'Now I know what that white horse is famous for.'

The first Wembley FA Cup final replay took place at Old Trafford on 29 April 1970 between Leeds and Chelsea. David Webb scored the winning goal for Chelsea in the 104th minute with a header.

Between 20 and 29 April 1912 West Bromwich Albion played seven matches, including an FA Cup final replay against Barnsley, without winning a game.

Bill Slater, footballer of the year in 1960 and whose birthday is on 29 April, is the brother of Maureen Flowers, one of Britain's leading female darts players.

In the 1936/37 season Joe Payne of Luton and Ted Harston of Mansfield set up Division III (North) and (South) scoring records, both with fifty-five goals.

S. Wynne, playing full-back for Bury on 30 April 1928, collapsed while taking a free kick against Sheffield United at Brammall Lane and died in the dressing-room. Death was diagnosed as being due primarily to pneumonia.

Between 1900 and 1902 Southampton reached two FA Cup finals as a non-League club. In 1900 they lost 0–4 to Bury and after drawing 1–1 with Sheffield United in 1902, lost 1–2 in the replay.

Mick Channon of Southampton was the leading goal-scorer in Division I in 1973/74 with twenty-one goals, in spite of which his club was still relegated. A similar fate befell Bob Hatton of Blackpool in the 1977/78 season when he scored twenty-two goals in Division II and still saw Blackpool drop a division.

Kick-off

The championships, promotions, relegations, and the joys and disappointments that go with them — everything in fact that makes Football League clubs and players go round, and up and down — come to a head in May.

Perhaps the most notable memory I have of that tense but exciting period at the close of the season was the marvellous occasion in 1966 when I was managing Coventry City, and we beat Wolverhampton Wanderers and entered Division One for the first time. There were fifty-one thousand packed into the ground that afternoon, including kids lined all round the pitch. Wolves scored first and it looked as if they were going to win. Then we scored an equalizer. All the kids who had been let on to the track at the edge of the pitch came on to the field. The commercial manager of the club, who also acted as our disc jockey, appealed to them over the public address system, telling them that Coventry City had a reputation for good behaviour and asking them not to let the team and club down. His appeal was given with the sort of carefully balanced emotion that I think would help with a lot of similar crowd disturbances today. Twenty years ago, it certainly did the trick with moving success. When we scored a second time, there was silence all round the ground as we all waited to see if the kids would do what they had been asked. Not one of them put a foot on the pitch.

To me, as manager, that one moment became almost more important than our final victory and subsequent championship at the top of the Division.

May

A farewell match to mark the retirement of the great West German player Uwe Seeler was arranged for 1 May 1972, the first time that any German player had been honoured in this way.

Millwall is the only London club not to have played in Division I.

In the 1919/20 season Darlington of the North Eastern League beat Sheffield Wednesday and so became the first non-League club to win on a Division I ground in the FA competition.

Denis Law is the only British player to have scored five hat-tricks in European competitions: 1963/64 Cup-winners' Cup (twice); 1964/65 European Fairs Cup; and 1968/69 European Cup (once in each leg).

On 2 May 1975 Alfie Conn of Spurs made his international debut for Scotland against Northern Ireland as a substitute, and in doing so emulated his father whose one Scottish international appearance was at Hampden Park in the 1956 match against Austria in which he scored the equalizing goal that gave a 1–1 draw.

Since Luton were without a manager at the time, their chairman, Thomas Hodgson, led them out at Wembley to contest the FA Cup final with Nottingham Forest on 2 May 1959.

When Arsenal beat Loughborough Town 12–0 in 1900 they established their record history as well as gained revenge for the 0–8 defeat they had suffered at the hands of Loughborough four years earlier.

3 May is the birthday of Len Shackleton, who in 1955 published his autobiography _Clown Prince of Soccer_, in which he left a blank page under the title 'What The Average Club Director Knows About Soccer'.

Arsenal's first leg of their League and FA Cup double in 1971 began with a match at White Hart Lane against Spurs on 3 May. Leeds had already completed their programme and had scored 64 points. Arsenal's tally was 63 points and they needed only a goal-less draw to win the title by 0.013 of a goal, but a defeat, or a goal-scoring draw would concede the championship to Leeds. An estimated 100,000 would-be spectators had to be locked out of the packed stadium. With three minutes to go, Ray Kennedy headed the only goal of the match, giving Arsenal victory. Five days later they beat Liverpool in the FA Cup final.

Thirty-one people died in the Turin air crash of 4 May 1949 including the team manager, Leslie Lievesely.

In 1975 Watford's player-manager Mike Keen was booked by referee Clive Thomas for handling the ball: it was Keen's 650th Football League match!

King George V became the first reigning monarch to attend an FA Cup final in 1914 when Burnley beat Liverpool 1-0 at Crystal Palace.

In 1975 Jim Cumbes of Aston Villa had the unique distinction of winning a Football League Cup winners' medal and County Cricket Championship medal for Worcestershire.

For many people the greatest football match ever played in Britain took place at Hampden Park on 5 May 1960, but it didn't involve a British side. It was the European Cup final between Eintracht Frankfurt and Real Madrid, who were seeking their fifth successive European Cup final victory. Eintracht were the first and last to score, but lost 3–7 to Real Madrid, who included players like Di Stefano, who scored three goals, and Puskas who got four.

Alan Mullery scored an own goal after just thirty seconds of a Division I game between Fulham and Sheffield Wednesday in 1961 by passing the ball backwards twenty yards without anyone else touching it.

In 1960 Cliff Holton scored hat-tricks two days running: on Good Friday against Chester and on Easter Saturday against Gateshead.

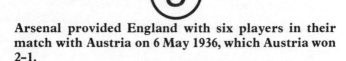

Arsenal provided England with six players in their match with Austria on 6 May 1936, which Austria won 2–1.

Graham Souness joined Middlesbrough from Spurs in 1974 without having played any League football for the London club.

Bromley won the FA Amateur Cup in 1949 and during the season their centre-forward, George Brown, scored 100 goals in all.

In 1973 Don Revie and Bob Stokoe were rival managers in the FA Cup final when Leeds played Sunderland, just as they had been opposing players eighteen years earlier — Revie with Manchester City and Stokoe with Newcastle.

7

Newcastle United won their third FA Cup final in five years by beating Manchester City 3–1 on 7 May 1955. B. Mitchell, J. Milburn and S. Cowell played on all three occasions.

Alan Oaks and Glyn Pardoe, who played in the Manchester City team that won the FA Cup in 1961, the European Cup-winners' Cup in 1970, became Division I champions in 1968 and won the League Cup in 1970, were cousins.

When Manchester United won the FA Cup in 1948 they played Division I clubs in every round: Aston Villa, who they beat 6–4; Liverpool, beaten 3–0; Charlton, 2–0; Preston, 4–1; Derby, 3–1 and Blackpool, beaten 4–2 in the final.

The Anglo-Italian Cup was founded in 1970 with Swindon Town its first winners. Swindon also won the first Anglo-Italian League Cup-winners' Cup in 1969.

8

The first abandoned international match in Scottish soccer was on 8 May 1963 in what was supposed to be a friendly with Austria. Before this meeting Scotland had beaten the Austrians just once in nine matches. With seventy-nine minutes of the match gone, with two Austrians sent off, and blatant fouling by the remaining players on the field, not to mention persistent protests by the Austrian management, the referee Jim Finney abandoned the game with Scotland winning 4–1.

When Rodney Marsh headed the winning goal for Fulham in a Division I match with Leicester City in 1963, it left him with permanent deafness.

England and Middlesex cricketers Patsy Hendren and Denis Compton also played wartime football internationals for England.

⑨

Colin Grainger scored twice in his England debut in the first England-Brazil match at Wembley on 9 May 1956. England won 4–2 and two penalties that were missed might have made it 6–2.

The first game of football that attracted any significant interest in Hungary was played on 9 May 1897 when a hundred spectators turned up to watch two of the Budapest Torna teams play on the Millanaris field.

In 1962 Ron Barnes, Wyn Davies and Roy Ambler each scored three goals for Wrexham in a 10–0 win against Hartlepool.

John Reynolds, who played League football in Ireland, Scotland and England, was also the first player to represent two different nations in international championships. He played five times for Ireland between 1890 and 1891 and eight times for England between 1892 and 1894.

⑩

England and Germany played their first international on 10 May 1930, a game that ended in a 3–3 draw. Germany had to wait thirty-eight years before gaining their first win as West Germany.

Both goalkeepers scored during a Scottish Division I match in 1910. Brownlie got his goal for Third Lanark and Hampton scored his for Motherwell.

In the 1960/61 season Bobby Smith not only featured in the Spurs side that achieved the double, but also played in all three of England's home international championships, equalling the feat of Charlie Athersmith of Aston Villa in 1897.

Sheffield United's Jim Iley missed two penalties in four minutes in a Division II match against Notts County in 1967.

When Italy beat Hungary 3–2 on 11 May 1947 all but one of the side played for Juventus.

FIFA was formed in 1904 with seven member countries: Belgium, Denmark, France, the Netherlands, Spain, Sweden and Switzerland. By 1972 there were 140 members.

During a match between Everton and Spurs at White Hart Lane in the 1924/25 season the Everton right-wing, Chedgzoy, took a corner kick and instead of crossing it, dribbled the ball into the Spurs penalty area and kicked it into the net, without playing it to a team mate. The referee's first reaction was to disallow the goal, but it was eventually allowed to stand because at that time no rule had been infringed. The present rule, that a player taking a corner kick must not be allowed to play the ball twice, was introduced later.

When England played Malta on 12 May 1971 at Wembley in the Nations Cup the England goalkeeper, Gordon Banks, did not receive the ball directly from a Maltese player once during the entire match, which England won 5–0.

W.G. Richardson, who scored 228 goals for West Bromwich Albion during the 1920s and 30s, added a G to his name to distinguish him from the Albion centre-half Bill Richardson.

During the Hungarian uprising of 1956 it was rumoured that the Hungarian football star Ferenc Puskas had been killed in the fighting. Fortunately these were unfounded rumours and Puskas went on to match a great playing career by managing the Greek club Panathinaikos to reach the European Cup final in 1971.

There is a club side in Chile called Everton.

On 13 May 1979 Perugia completed the season undefeated when they drew 2–2 against Bologna in their final Italian League match. However, they came second in the table to AC Milan.

The first time the FA Cup final was played in May was in 1937 when Sunderland beat Preston North End 3–1.

The Scottish League club Berwick Rangers has its ground, Shielfield Park, in England.

Nine Keetley brothers played professional football, including four for Donacaster Rovers in the 1920s. During six seasons Ted Keetley scored 180 goals.

The World Cup final of 1934 featured two goalkeeper captains, Combi of Italy and Palnicka of Czechoslovakia.

Sheffield Wednesday's Graham Pugh played in the 1966 FA Cup final on 14 May after making his League debut only five days before.

Between 1920 and 1927 Portsmouth became the first club to rise from Division III to Division I in the Football League.

The famous Raich Carter captained Sunderland just once, when they won the FA Cup in 1937.

William 'Fatty' Foulke, one of the great characters of football at the turn of the century, was a twenty-stone goalkeeper who played in FA Cup finals for Sheffield United in 1899, 1901 and 1902. In 1905 he became Chelsea's first Football League goalkeeper and later joined Bradford after putting on more weight and touching twenty-three stone.

William Fatty Foulke, one of the great characters of football.

May

England suffered their first defeat by a foreign team on 15 May 1929 when they were beaten 3–4 by Spain in Madrid. They gained revenge two years later at Highbury when they won 7–1.

On 15 May 1971 Leeds United had eight players in the home international championship: Madeley, Cooper and Clarke for England; Lorimer, Bremner and Gray for Scotland; and Sprake and Yorath for Wales.

Ipswich entered the Football League in 1938 replacing Gillingham, but Gillingham regained their Football League status in 1950.

In 1972 Bournemouth moved alphabetically to first place in the Football League by changing their name from Bournemouth and Boscombe Athletic to AFC Bournemouth.

An England tour of Scandinavia in the middle of May 1937 produced an impressive list of wins: England beat Norway 6–0, Sweden 4–0 and Finland 8–0, in which match Freddie Steele scored seven goals; in fact he scored eight goals in six internationals.

During the 1956/57 season there were eleven victories by non-League clubs over League clubs.

Between 1894 and 1899 Oldham Athletic were known as Pine Villa.

Ronnie Rooke was playing with Fulham at the age of thirty-five in 1947 and was contemplating retirement when he joined Arsenal and found himself the top scorer in the Football League the following year with thirty-three goals.

Colin Stein was the last Scot to score four goals in an international when Scotland beat Cyprus 8-0 in a World Cup qualifying match on 17 May 1969.

On 17 May 1959 Seminario of Peru became the last player to score a hat-trick against England in an international.

When Bob Stokoe was with Rochdale in 1968 in his early days as a manager, he gave eleven players free transfers, sold the goalkeeper Les Green to Derby for £8,000 and with the money bought nine players, four sets of team strip and a fresh coat of paint for the ground.

There are three Football League clubs that have their home grounds outside their home towns: Grimsby, Manchester United and Nottingham Forest.

The first time that England used a substitute in an international was in the match against Belgium on 18 May 1950 when Wolves' Jimmy Mullen went on in place of the injured Jackie Milburn. Mullen scored one of England's goals that gave them a 4-1 victory.

One of the most exciting promotion matches of all time occurred in Division II on 18 May 1963 when Sunderland, second in the division, played against Chelsea who were only one place behind. Chelsea won 1-0 with a goal by Tommy Harmer, the only goal he scored in Division II in a seventeen-year career. Chelsea bounced back into Division I, but Sunderland had to wait until the following year before gaining their promotion.

After being admitted to the Football League in the 1920/21 season, Southend United had to wait fifty-one years before winning their first promotion, from Division IV to Division III.

Bill Nicholson, the future of Spurs 'double' manager, played in his only England international on 19 May 1951. Positioned at right-half, he scored one of the goals that gave England their 5–2 victory over Portugal at Wembley.

When Leeds became Division II champions in 1964 Paul Madeley played in every position except in goal.

Albert Ironmonger played his last match for Notts County at the end of the 1925/26 season, having made 563 previous appearances for the club. That game proved to be a 'last' for Notts County too because they were relegated from Division I and did not return until over fifty years later in 1981. (Ironmonger was also a county cricketer who played nineteen times for Nottinghamshire).

In May 1974 Stockport County sacked their manager Brian Doyle because he lived sixty miles from Stockport.

Bobby Charlton scored his last and forty-ninth England goal against Columbia on 20 May 1970 when England won 4–0 in Bogota.

In the 1982/83 season Portsmouth became the first club to win Division II twice: the other occasion had been in 1961/62.

Huddersfield became the first Division I champions to play in Division IV after successive relegations.

Sir Matt Busby managed the Great Britain team in the 1948 Olympic Games.

Gillingham's goalkeeper Fred Fox holds the club's record as its most capped player when he made his one appearance for England on 21 May 1925. He was selected to play for England when with Gillingham, but had actually been transferred to Millwall before the match with France in Paris on 21 May 1925. As it was, he was injured during the first half and was replaced by Billy Walker after half-time.

The Liverpool full-back Ephraim Longworth was the first Liverpool player to captain England in an international in the 1920s.

CSKA Sophia has won a record twenty-one post-war national league titles in Bulgaria.

The Metropolitan Police Five-a-Side Youth competition in 1981 attracted an entry of 7,008 teams.

George Best was born on 22 May 1946 and twenty-two years later, only a few days before his birthday, he became the youngest Footballer of the Year.

In 1971 Reading celebrated its club centenary by being relegated to Division IV for the first time in its history.

J. Fallon was the first player to be awarded a testimonial by Clydebank, in 1983.

In the 1972/73 season Willie Carlin won promotion with his fourth successive club, achieving this feat with Notts County, Carlisle, Derby County and Leicester.

Kurt Hampin scored in his third European Cup-winners' Cup final on 23 May 1968. That afternoon he scored for AC Milan in their match against Hamburg, having previously scored for Fiorentina in the 1961 and 1962 finals.

The longest player-manager relationship lasted twenty-two years between 1934 and 1956 when Charlton's manager Jimmy Seed and player Sam Bartram served the club during 583 league games.

Jimmy Furnell is possibly the only player to become a professional footballer via the labour exchange. When signing on he was asked what job he would like and told the clerk 'a footballer'. He was put in touch with Burnley for whom he played twice, before moving to Liverpool, Arsenal, Rotherham and Plymouth.

George Best, born on 22 May 1946, was the youngest Footballer of the Year.

May

In spite of an impressive career with three London clubs, Chelsea, Queen's Park Rangers and Arsenal, over 600 Football League appearances, playing in the European Cup-winners' Cup finals of 1971 with Chelsea and 1980 with Arsenal, John Hollins made only one international appearance for England. That was on 24 May 1967 in the match against Spain which England won 2-0.

George Young who played for Rangers and Scotland in the 1940s and 50s was nicknamed Corkey because he always carried the cork from the champagne bottle that Rangers had opened to celebrate their 1948 Scottish Cup victory over Morton.

Terry Butcher, who won his first international cap for England against Australia in 1980, was born in Singapore.

When Jock Stein's Celtic surprised Inter-Milan and won the European Cup on 25 May 1967 they broke an eleven-year Latin stronghold on the cup.

Alan Birchinall was the first footballer to be transferred for £100,000 on three separate occasions: from Sheffield United to Chelsea, to Crystal Palace and to Leicester.

Manchester United fielded a complete team of internationals during the 1966/67 season: Gregg (Northern Ireland), Brennan and Dunne (Republic of Ireland), Crerand (Scotland), Foulkes and Stiles (England), Best (Northern Ireland), Law (Scotland), Charlton (England), Herd (Scotland) and Connolly (England).

The first FA Cup final in which nets were used was the one played between Blackburn Rovers and Notts County in 1891.

'I don't think it's that kind of net we're supposed to use, George.'

When Norman Whiteside scored for Manchester United in the FA Cup final on 26 May 1983 he was just eighteen years nineteen days old, the youngest player to score during an FA Cup final.

A forty-two year old fitter named Dick Broadbent paid a price for rashly predicting that Grimsby Town would not get promoted from Division IV that season. Grimsby had had to apply for re-election at the end of the previous season, so his hunch seemed well founded. Unfortunately for Mr Broadbent, Grimsby headed Division IV in 1972 and he found himself having to run naked round his firm's yard as he had pledged to do. Grimsby's manager Lawrie McMenemy presented him with a certificate as a memento of the occasion.

When Northern Ireland beat Italy 2–1 to enter their first World Cup finals in 1958 it was also the first time that Italy had failed to qualify for the final stages of the competition.

Egypt played their only World Cup finals match on 27 May 1934, losing 2–4 to Hungary.

In 1973 Matt Gillies, then manager of Nottingham Forest, was the first to sell four players for over £100,000: Terry Hennessey to Derby for £110,000 in 1970; Henry Newton to Everton in 1970 for £130,000; Ian Storey Moore to Manchester United in 1972 for £120,000; and Peter Cormack to Liverpool in 1972 for £110,000.

Following Arsenal's 0–1 defeat in the 1927 FA Cup final their goalkeeper Dan Lewis blamed his new jersey. Since then all Arsenal goalkeepers have washed their new jerseys before playing in them.

In the 1931/32 season Motherwell's William McFadyen established a record of fifty-two goals in the Scottish League Division I.

When Belfast Celtic were touring the USA in May 1949 they played the Scottish national team at Triborough Stadium in New York and beat them 2–0.

Robert 'Rabbi' Howell is the only gipsy to have played international football for England. While he was with Liverpool he played in the England-Ireland match of 1895 and four years later was picked to play against Scotland.

Apart from 0–0 draws with England in 1958 and Czechoslovakia in 1962, Brazil had a run of thirteen consecutive World Cup victories.

The first player to be sent off in a Scottish FA Cup final was Jack Buchanan of Rangers in 1929. Aitken of Celtic matched this when he was sent off in the 1984 final.

Tom Finney played his last match for Preston against Luton Town at the end of May 1960. Luton were relegated and Preston finished ninth in the League. The following year they finished their first season without Tom Finney twenty-first in the League and have never since returned to that high point.

Dave Thomas, who played for Burnley and Queen's Park Rangers in the 1970s, had a grandfather who once featured in a penalty shoot-out with an elephant and won 11–2.

Sunderland became the first Football League club to score 100 Football League goals when they reached that total in 1893.

Birmingham City had four international goalkeepers on their books in 1929: Harry Hibbs, R. Tremling, S. Swater and Ken Tewksbury.

A standard scale of payment for referees was established on 30 May 1938. The fee for a League game was set at three guineas and linesmen were to be given a guinea and a half.

In their early days Bolton Wanderers wore red and white quartered shirts which gave them the nickname the Reds. In about 1883 they tried different colour schemes including loose white shirts with red spots, which it was claimed made their players look bigger.

Stoke City made the largest profit in the Football League in the first post-Second World War season with £32,207.

Ted McDougall scored his first hundred goals for Bournemouth in just 122 games. When at one stage he went for a run of five games without scoring the press reported it as 'a famine'.

J. Kendall scored a hat-trick when he made his Football League debut for Barrow against Rotherham United on 31 May 1947.

Chesterfield, the last Football League club to acquire floodlights, finally 'switched on' in the 1968/69 season.

During the 1950s Crystal Palace became the first Football League club to appoint a female secretary, Margaret Montague.

During the 1945/46 season Jimmy Scoular played for both Gosport and Portsmouth in the FA Cup.

Kick-off

This is probably the one month in the year when football players and managers can look forward to a rest. For television commentators the World Cup can provide stimulating work once every four years. In 1966 I was covering the final with Joe Mercer for the BBC and we were both in tears when England finally clinched their historic victory. Four years later, I was with ITV in Mexico, seeing the dazzling performance of the Brazilians and a wonderful carnival background to some memorable football. The passage of time means that these memories stand out more than some of the disappointments, like England's defeat by West Germany and the subsequent (and I think unjustified) criticism of Alf Ramsey's decision to make substitutions, most notably of Bobby Charlton. But with England leading by two goals at one point in the game, it seemed clear that he intended resting Charlton for the final — which I considered an astute and eminently sensible decision. Unfortunately, West Germany made substitutions of their own and capitalized on them — but that is part of the fascination of football!

June

On 1 June 1931 the Football League decided at its annual meeting not to allow the broadcasting of any League matches. This ban was not lifted until 1937 when permission was given for certain games to be broadcast on overseas wavelengths.

In June 1862 J.C. Thring, a master at Uppingham School, drew up one of the earliest codes of football rules for what he called 'the simplest game'.

Two Bells set up records at Tranmere Rovers: during the 1933/34 season Bunney Bell scored thirty-five goals; he also scored the highest aggregate of goals between 1931 and 1936 with a total of 104, while between 1946 and 1964 Harold Bell made a record 595 appearances for the club.

Maurice Setters played in sixteen Under-23 internationals for England between 1958 and 1960 without once winning a full England Cap.

Manchester United paid £11,000 for Reg Allen when they bought him from Queen's Park Rangers in June 1950, so making him the first goalkeeper to be transferred for over £10,000.

A publican named Richard Payne offered to hypnotize the entire Oldham Athletic team when they were struggling at the bottom of Division II in the 1953/54 season. His idea was to induce confidence into the players but the offer was refused by the club manager who commented that they might have been 'desperate, but not that desperate'.

The night before a crucial game against Dundee United in 1934 Murdie Wallace of Albion Rovers dreamt that he scored the winning goal that gained promotion for his side. The following afternoon his dream came true — he scored the goal and Albion were duly promoted.

3

The birthday of Ken Armstrong, the former Chelsea and England player of the mid-1950s who emigrated to New Zealand where he became the national director of coaching.

The 1907/08 season ended with Arsenal and Blackburn Rovers finishing equal fourteenth in Division I with identical records. Both sides had played thirty-eight games, won twelve, drawn twelve, lost fourteen, scored fifty-one goals and both had conceded sixty-three goals. The result was that both ended with thirty-six points.

The first Bolivian League champions, in 1914, were a team called 'The Strongest'.

The Scottish League club Stranraer, which was formed in 1870, went for 108 of its first 110 years without a manager. The team was picked on Monday nights by the club's twelve directors.

4

Norway scored their first victory over one of the home international countries when they beat Scotland 4–3 in Bergen on 4 June 1963.

Albania did not play one of the home countries until as recently as 1965 when they were grouped with Northern Ireland in a World Cup qualifying competition.

There are few sportsmen who have won major honours in football and cricket but Harry Makepeace of Everton and Lancashire achieved a remarkable record in both games. He was in Everton's League-winning side of 1906 and the championship side of 1915. In addition he was capped four times for England between 1906 and 1912. As a cricketer he was a member of Lancashire's championship side in 1926, scoring 2,340 runs in his forty-sixth year. In 1920/21 he played in four test matches in Australia, scoring 117 at Melbourne.

On 5 June 1968 Alan Mullery became the first English international to be sent off, during a match against Yugoslavia.

One of the world's stormiest competitions, the World Club Championships, which featured the European Cup champions against the South American champions, resulted in a clash between Celtic and the Argentinian side Racing Club in 1967. Celtic won the first leg at Parkhead 1–0. Racing took the second leg 2–1, and all square they went to Montevideo to play the decider. There tempers frayed and six men were sent off (four Celtic players and two from Racing). Racing won 1–0 and each player was presented with £2,000 and a new car. The Celtic players, on the other hand were each fined £250 by the club's board of directors.

England's match against Austria on 6 June 1908 was the first official international between any of the home countries and a foreign national team.

When Charles Buchan joined Arsenal from Sunderland in 1925 his initial fee was £2,000. In addition he was offered £100 for every goal he scored that season — he scored twenty-one and earned himself a total fee of £4,100.

To celebrate the opening of their new stadium at Ibrox Park, Rangers invited the English double champions Preston to play against them and lost 1–8.

Uwe Seller of West Germany played his twenty-first and last World Cup finals match in 1970.

⑦

Stranraer were the last Scottish League Club to install flood-lighting when they completed their system in June 1981.

Ray Straw of Derby County and Coventry City is believed to be the only player to have played in all six divisions, between 1952 and 1960.

Between 1913 and 1932 Huddersfield were unbeaten at home in twenty-six FA Cup ties, losing eventually to Arsenal.

During a Mexican League match Carlos Zomba scored four goals for Atlanta against Los Apaches. As he left the ground at the end of the game a Los Apaches fan drew a gun and shot him four times in the legs — one shot for each goal. Zomba never played again.

⑧

The first time England faced the USA after a humiliating defeat at the hands of the Americans in the 1950 World Cup competition was on 8 June 1953. England made certain of victory on this occasion, winning 6–3 in New York.

In 1978 Robbie James of Swansea became the youngest player to have played in 200 Football League matches (he was also the youngest to have played in 100).

One of Dundee United's early heroes was their centre-forward Duncan Hutchison who was hotly pursued by many Football League clubs until he was eventually sold to Newcastle United. To show their loyalty, 300 Dundee supporters journeyed to St James's Park to see his debut, and before the game they went on to the pitch to present him with good luck tokens.

On 9 June Djalma Santos made his 107th and final appearance for Brazil in their match against Uruguay; Brazil won 2-0.

During the 1977/78 season eleven players represented Tranmere Rovers in forty-one of their forty-six matches. The first team change did not come until the twenty-ninth League game that season.

According to the rule governing the dimensions of the ball, its circumference must not exceed twenty-eight inches and must not be less than twenty-seven, and it must weigh between fourteen and sixteen ounces.

In 1912 Lincoln City became the first winners of the Central League.

England registered only their second victory over Brazil on 10 June 1984 when they beat them 2-0 with goals by Barnes and Hateley. The previous success had been the first meeting between the two countries when England won 4-2 at Wembley in 1956.

In finishing as top goal-scorer in the Football League with thirty goals in the 1977/78 season Bob Latchford won a prize offered by the *Daily Express* to any player who scored thirty or more goals in either Division I or Division II that season.

In 1978 Willie Bell resigned from Lincoln City to go on a religious crusade in the USA.

The idea behind the FA Cup competition came from Charles Alcock whose old school, Harrow, had a simple knock-out competition among the houses, with the winner being known as the 'cock house'.

Allan Clarke has three good reasons for remembering this date and in 1970 they all came together. That afternoon he scored from the penalty spot in his England debut during a World Cup match against Czechoslovakia, adding another highlight to a day that was also his wife's birthday and their wedding anniversary.

In 1979 Norwich City drew a record number of twenty-three Division I matches.

In the 1979 Varsity match Cambridge's Maurice Cox scored the fastest goal at Wembley and the following year, while a professional with Torquay, he became the first professional footballer to play in the Varsity match.

In 1953 Raich Carter came out of retirement and won an Irish Cup winners' medal with Cork.

Clive Allen joined Arsenal from Queen's Park Rangers on 12 June 1980, stayed two months and then moved to Crystal Palace without playing a match for Arsenal.

The Cheshire Schoolboy half-back line of the early 1930s all became England internationals in later life. The boys picked for Cheshire were Stan Cullis, Joe Mercer and Frank Soo.

The Old Carthusians were the only team to win both the Amateur Cup (in 1897) and the FA Cup (in 1881).

The first international played in Europe between two non-British sides was the match between Austria and Hungary which the Austrians won 5–0.

Between 13 June and 11 July 1982 over two million spectators in seventeen sportsgrounds spread over fourteen cities and towns in Spain watched the World Cup finals.

Bill Shankly once missed a penalty against Liverpool in front of the Kop when he was playing for Preston North End.

Between 1950 and 1966 Helenio Herrera won national league championships as manager of three different clubs: Atletico Madrid, Barcelona and Inter Milan.

Frank Dudley's first three Football League goals in the 1953/54 season were scored for three different clubs, in three different divisions: Southend, Division III (South); Cardiff, Division I and Brentford, Division II.

Swindon Town's John Trollope, born on 14 June 1943, made a record number of Football League appearances for a single club between 1961 and 1980: 770. His final game was against Colchester in October 1980.

When Wilf Smith played for England Youth against Belgium in 1965 he was the first German-born player to wear an England shirt. He was born in Nuemunster in 1946.

The Scottish League and Cup have seldom been won by non-Glasgow clubs: in 1895 St Bernards won the Cup and Hearts the League; in 1952 Motherwell won the Cup and Hibernian the League; in 1955 Clyde won the Cup and Aberdeen the League; in 1958 Clyde again won the cup and Hearts took the League title; in 1983 Aberdeen won the Cup and Dundee won the League title; and in 1984 Aberdeen won both the Cup and the League.

On 15 June 1972 Rangers' manager, Willie Waddell, had to plead with the UEFA disciplinary committee to let Rangers keep the UEFA cup. Following their 3–2 victory over Moscow Dynamo on 24 May thousands of Rangers fans went on the rampage in Barcelona where the match had been played.

In 1952 and 1954 Spain became the International Youth champions, winning on both occasions by the toss of a coin.

In 1950 Liverpool provided the England centre-half for successive international matches. On 14 May W.H. Jones played against Belgium in Brussels and on 15 June L. Hughes played against Chile in Rio in a World Cup match.

In 1971 Carlisle United became the first club to sell its manager to another club when Bob Stokoe was bought by Blackpool.

Bryan Robson scored the earliest goal in any World Cup match on 16 June 1982, twenty-seven seconds after the start of England's match against France in Bilbao. In the twenty-fourth minute of the same match Peter Shilton let in a goal, though after that he prevented any further shots getting past him in the matches against Czechoslovakia, Kuwait, West Germany and Spain.

Steve Bloomer was one of the great goal-scorers of the early years of this century. His 352 Football League goals for Derby County and Middlesbrough between 1892 and 1914 set a record that remained unbroken until Dixie Dean passed it in the late 1930s. Bloomer's scoring record for England (twenty-eight goals) lasted until broken by Nat Lofthouse and Tom Finney in the late 1950s.

Jimmy Dickinson had the great misfortune on 17 June 1954 of being the only Englishman to score an own goal in a World Cup match. The lucky side on that occasion was Belgium.

'If Agatha Christie had written the script you could not have done better for a thriller,' said Tommy Docherty of the match between Italy and West Germany in the 1970 World Cup finals on 17 June. After ninety minutes this semi-final looked like remaining at a 1-1 draw. However, the match burst into life in extra time and in the next half hour five goals were scored, with Italy squeezing ahead by a goal at 3-2, only to be equalized by a goal from Muller, before Riva finally gave Italy their 4-3 victory and a place in the final.

Between 1920 and 1922 Bradford dropped from Division I to Division III in successive seasons.

East Germany made their World Cup debut on 18 June 1974 in a match against Chile. The game was played in West Berlin but only a party of carefully selected East Germans, 3,020 in all, were allowed to cross from East Berlin to see the game.

Manchester United recorded their greatest club victory against worthy opposition when they beat Anderlecht 10-0 in a World Cup preliminary round in 1956.

Johnny Duncan, who was manager at Don Revie's first club, Leicester City, also became his father-in-law.

At one time the Gaelic Athletic Association in Ireland imposed a ban under Rule 27 that none of their members could play the 'alien' (ie: English) games of football, cricket, rugby or hockey. The approved sports were Gaelic football or hurling.

'Sean, have you been playing those Alien games?'

On 19 June 1965 an experimental game with no offside decisions was played between Heart of Midlothian and Kilmarnock. Hearts won 8–2.

Dixie Dean scored sixty goals in the 1927/28 season, beating George Camsell's record by one goal. At the start of his crucial game against Arsenal Dean needed a hat-trick to pass Camsell's record that had been set the previous year. He achieved this seemingly outside chance in spite of the Gunners scoring twice. Not only did Dixie Dean establish a new record that afternoon, Everton also clinched the League title.

Middlesbrough first gained professional status in 1889, but three years later they reverted to amateur status, after which they won the amateur cup from 1895 to 1898 and the following year were admitted to Division II.

The European Nations Cup final on 20 June 1976 was the first major championship to be decided by a penalty shoot-out, following a 2–2 draw between Czechoslovakia and West Germany. The penalties were level at 3–3 when West Germany's Willi Hoeness kicked his shot straight into the crowd, allowing Panenka to take the title for Czechoslovakia with the winning shot.

The first British player to play Italian League football after 1945 was Arsenal's T. Sloan.

Among the casualties in the British footballing world in the Second World War were Liverpool's full-back Tommy Cooper, who was killed while serving as a dispatch rider; Harry Coslin, Bolton Wanderers' pre-war captain, killed in action in Italy; and Luton's goalkeeper Cohan, shot down over the Ruhr.

Spain played the USSR in the final of the European Nations Cup on 21 June 1964 and won 2–1. Four years earlier they had withdrawn on political grounds as a protest against Russian involvement in the Spanish Civil War a quarter of a century earlier.

The first substitute to be called on during a World Cup final was the Italian player Juliano, who replaced his team mate Bertini, in their 1–4 defeat by Brazil on 21 June 1970.

Only seventy years before the era of million-pound transfer fees Alf Common became the first four-figure player when he moved from Sunderland to Middlesbrough for £1,000 in February 1905. The previous year he had been the first player to change clubs for more than £500 when he moved to Sunderland from Sheffield United for £520.

'Hey, Luigi, I said bring on the substitute!'

On 22 June 1937 Joe Louis won the world heavyweight boxing championship and retained it for over eleven years until his retirement in 1949. One of his lesser known sporting achievements was signing professional forms for Liverpool in 1944.

Football was introduced into the Olympic Games in 1900 in Paris, when Upton Park, representing Great Britain, beat France 4–0 in an exhibition match.

Hughie Gallagher, scorer of 386 goals in British League football and capped seventeen times for Scotland, once turned down the opportunity to play for the national team in order to help Newcastle fight off relegation.

Between 1907 and 1914 Blackburn's Bob Crompton and West Brom's Jessie Pennington played together in twenty-three of the thirty-one home international championships.

Following a game in Argentina between River Plate and Arch-Gival Baca Junior on 23 June 1968, the crowd stampeded and seventy-one spectators were killed and 200 injured.

Newcastle United's Irish International Billy McCracken, who played for the club during the 1920s and became known as a master tactician, was largely responsible for the change in the offside rule in 1925.

Following the closure of their Meadowside Park ground in 1906, Partick Thistle played at Ibrox Park, Rangers' home ground, for twelve months before moving to their current ground, Firhill. Ironically it was Rangers they beat in 1921 to win their first trophy, the Scottish FA Cup.

In 1884 Oswestry became the first team to take the Welsh Cup out of Wales.

The fourth World Cup final competition began on 24 June 1950 with Brazil, the hosts, winning the opening match against Mexico 4–0.

Tony Book and Francis Lee, who later teamed up at Manchester City, confronted each other earlier in their careers in an FA Cup tie when Bolton, Lee's club at the time, was drawn against non-League Bath, for whom Book was playing. A member of the Bolton training staff was sent to spy on Bath and reported back, 'They've got an old full-back who is very dodgy. Play on him and it should be easy.' So Bolton concentrated their game on Tony Book and were lucky to escape with a draw.

Dave Mackay played his fortieth cup final at all levels when Spurs met Chelsea in the FA Cup final in 1967. Mackay never played on the losing side in any of these matches.

The match between Chile and Uruguay on 25 June 1975 was abandoned after eighty minutes following a fight on the pitch that led to the sending off of nine Uruguayans and all but one of the Chilean side.

One wartime fixture at Stamford Bridge between Chelsea and Charlton had to be abandoned because of fog that was so dense that Charlton's goalkeeper, Sam Bartram, remained in his goal for a good ten minutes after everyone else had left the pitch until a policeman appeared out of the mist and told him.

In the 1935/36 season Sunderland conceded seventy-four goals, a record by any Division I champions.

The first floodlit game in Great Britain was staged as long ago as 1878 at Bramall Lane, when two sides chosen by the Sheffield Association played each other.

The England touring team that played three tests against New Zealand in 1937 completed their hat-trick of victories with a 12–1 win in Wellington on 26 June. New Zealand's goal in that match was their only one of the tour in which England scored thirty.

Kilmarnock was founded in 1869 by a group of enthusiastic cricketers.

In 1964 Swansea City, lying nineteenth in Division II, reached the FA Cup semi-final with a 2–1 victory over Liverpool, in the year when they were League champions. The Liverpool fans began to exact their revenge on the Swansea goalkeeper, Noel Dwyer, before the end of the match and he collected three shillings in pennies and halfpennies thrown at him from the terraces. He kept this safely in his cap inside the goal, but in the excitement of the finish, someone pinched it.

The notorious 'Battle of Berne', a World Cup quarter-final between Hungary and Brazil, was played on 27 June 1954. The English referee, Arthur Ellis, had to send off three players: Santos and Tozzo of Brazil and Boszik of Hungary.

When Huddersfield won Division IV in 1980 they became the last Football League club to score over 100 goals in a season.

A century ago a season ticket to watch West Bromwich Albion cost three shillings (15 pence).

Between 1964 and 1971 Wales played forty internationals, but only three of them featured the teams that had originally been selected.

Eric Gates, who started his Football League career
with Ipswich in 1972, was born on 28 June 1955.

A Turkish belly dancer named Sether Seniz was so keen that
her national side should beat the West Germans in a forth-
coming international she offered her own special reward to
the first player to get the ball past the German goalkeeper.
This caused considerable discontent in the Turkish national
squad. The defenders thought they had been unfairly treated
and the goalkeeper was said to be skulking in the dressing-
room before the match. Whether any of the Germans
contemplated scoring an own goal is not recorded.

In June 1924 the rule was introduced that in cases where the
colours of the teams clashed in Football League fixtures, the
visitors would have to change to other colours.

England suffered one of their most humiliating
defeats on 29 June 1950, when they lost 1–0 to the USA
in the World Cup finals in Brazil.

In the 1892/93 and 1897/98 seasons test matches were played
to determine the promotion and relegation places between
Division I and II. The bottom three teams in Division I
played the top three teams in Division II.

Charlie Athersmith, a member of Aston Villa's double-
winning side of 1897, once played an entire League match
under an umbrella.

The Duke of Devonshire is President of Chesterfield Football
Club.

The day after the first anniversary of their humiliating defeat by the USA, England scored their record win when they beat Australia 17–0 on 30 June 1951.

Tom Whittaker, Arsenal's manager and later trainer of the 1920s and 1930s, introduced a forty-five-minute clock at Highbury, only to have it banned by the FA.

During the 1981/82 season Woodward Wanderers of the West Bromwich Youth League conceded 422 goals in eighteen matches and scored just four.

The trophy given to the winners of the FA Sunday Cup competition was originally donated by the Shah of Iran.

Kick-off

July is the start of the training slog for all footballers. Some clubs believe in starting earlier than others, but they are all well into their programmes by the end of the month.

I always looked on pre-season training as a very important part of a club's year. As a manager I saw those four weeks as setting the theme for the whole season, both physically and mentally.

I suspect players today come back a good deal fitter than many of them did in my time, but there is still work to be done: sharpening up, the re-learning of last season's tactics, and the planned systems for dealing with dead balls, free kicks and similar situations. Once the season starts, there is very little time for this kind of rehearsal when you are playing two matches a week, and there are inevitably one or two players injured and receiving treatment.

As a player I loved running, and Johnny Hayes and I used to run from Fulham over Putney Bridge on a circuit that brought us back up over Wimbledon Hill. It was quite a long route, and after one session we even drove it in a car to measure it because we thought we had broken a world record!

There was golf, too. Frank Osborne, Fulham's general manager in those days, could always be persuaded to have a game and we quickly convinced ourselves that at the end of a morning and afternoon of fairly strenuous pre-season training, golf was good because it relaxed us for the next day's sessions. So we would shoot off in the evenings and play eighteen holes. I wish I could still do that today!

July

In July 1959 the Football League established a copyright on their fixture list.

When Notts Forest beat the Irish club Linfield in the 1889 FA Cup competition, they became the only team to play sides from all four home countries in the competition.

When Brazil won their third World Cup in 1970 Jairzino scored in every round.

Dennis Wilshaw became the first man to score four goals in an international at Wembley when England beat Scotland 7–0 in 1954.

Barry Swallow, born on 2 July 1942, made 510 Football League appearances between 1960 and 1976 and missed only two games for York City in the seasons when they were promoted to Division III (1970/71) and to Division II (1973/74).

Arsenal's Eddie Kelly became the first substitute to score in an FA Cup final when he kicked an equalizer in the 1971 match against Liverpool.

The Welsh international Dick Roose played in goal twenty-three times for his country between 1899 and 1911. A doctor by profession, he played for whichever club was nearest his practice, representing Aberystwyth, London Welsh, Stoke, Everton, Sunderland, Aston Villa and Arsenal. When Wales were reduced to ten men during one match, Roose refused to draw a man out of the attack and went out of the goal himself to play both back and goalkeeper.

3 July is the birthday of Tommy Robson who scored over 100 goals in his career that lasted until past his thirty-fifth birthday.

The terrible winter weather of 1963 delayed the FA Cup final between Manchester United and Leicester City by three weeks as the backlog of lost games was made up.

Before Hugh McIlmoyle played for his first Scottish League club, Morton, in 1973/74 and became their top scorer with eight goals, he had played for eight clubs in the Football League.

John White, a member of Tottenham Hotspur's double-winning side of 1960/61, was killed by lightning on a golf course at Enfield in 1964.

This day is the anniversary of an important legal ruling that had widespread implications for professional footballers. On 4 July 1963 Mr Justice Wilberforce ruled on the case that followed George Eastham's application for a transfer from Newcastle, which was refused by the club according to the old retain-and-transfer system. This was brought to an end by the judge's ruling, 'The rules of the Football Association and regulations of the Football League relating to the retention and transfer of players of professional football, including the plaintiff, are not binding upon the plaintiff and are an unreasonable restraint of trade.'

On 4 July 1954 Hungary's record run of twenty-nine international matches without defeat was brought to an end after lasting since 14 May 1950.

July

Scotland played their first away game against Brazil on 5 July 1972 and were beaten 0-1 in Rio.

In 1921 the rule was introduced that goalkeepers in international matches had to wear yellow jerseys.

Bjorn Nordqvist was capped 115 times for Sweden between 1963 and 1978, setting a record for full international appearances.

In 1984 Forfar Athletic celebrated their centenary by winning the first football honours in their history, when they became Scottish League Division II champions.

Joe Wilson, who made 504 appearances for Workington, Nottingham Forest, Wolverhampton Wanderers and Newport County between 1955 and 1973, was born on 6 July 1937.

When Northern Ireland won the home international championships with a 1-1 draw against Wales in 1980, it was the first time they had won the competition outright since 1914.

In 1901 Sandy Brown of Spurs became the first player to score in every round of the FA Cup and his tally of fifteen goals remains a record.

A newspaper once described George Best as the 'Terry Conroy of Manchester'. Conroy was the star Stoke player of the late 1960s and early 70s who was capped twenty-six times for the Republic of Ireland.

'*I think one of us should tell our keeper that the yellow jersey is for tomorrow's international!*'

The opening day of the first Ladies' World Cup was 7 July 1970 when six nations took part in the final competition: Denmark, England, France, Italy, Mexico and West Germany.

After Gordon Banks had saved a shot from Pele during England's match against Brazil in the 1907 World Cup finals Pele commented, 'That was the greatest save I have ever seen by the greatest goalkeeper I have ever seen.'

In 1977 Wales gained their first victory over England since 1936 when goals by Astley and Jones secured a 2–1 victory at Molyneux.

Gerry Byrne played full-back for Liverpool for 117 minutes of the 1965 FA Cup final with a broken collar bone.

Mike Barnard, born on 8 July 1933, was an all-round sportsman for his county. As well as playing for Portsmouth between 1953 and 1958, he was a member of the county's first-class cricket side.

The FA Cup quarter-final in which Manchester City beat Stoke City 1–0 in 1934 attracted a record crowd for any FA Cup match other than a final: 84,569.

In 1972 Brentford's directors won a civil action against the accusation made by one newspaper that in selling Roger Cross to Fulham for £30,000 the board had betrayed the fans. The Brentford answer, upheld by the judge, was that they were merely honouring a pledge made to Cross that he would be allowed to better his chances in the game if the opportunity arose.

Graham Shaw, who played for Sheffield United and Doncaster Rovers in the 1950s and 60s, and who was also the England ABA Junior boxing champion and a cricketer for the Yorkshire Colts, was born on 9 July 1934.

West Ham's FA Cup-winning team of 1964 contained seven players with surnames that began with B: Bond, Burkett, Bovington, Brown, Brabrook, Boyce and Byrne.

All but one of the Spurs team that won the 1967 FA Cup final were international players.

Geoff Hurst became the last player to score six goals in a Football League Division I match, when he achieved this against Sunderland in 1968.

On 10 July 1978 Keith Burkinshaw signed the two Argentinian internationals Ardiles and Villa for £325,000 for Tottenham Hotspur.

Herbert Chapman, who managed both Arsenal and Huddersfield to their Division I hat-tricks, used to wear lemon-coloured boots when he was a player.

West Ham United's players Billy Bonds and Harry Redknapp were partners together in racing greyhounds.

In 1954 Preston North End's Joe Marston became the first Australian to play in an FA Cup final.

On 11 July 1925 Australia met England at Maitland and lost 8–2, but they still scored their highest total in that England tour.

The second FA Cup final between the Wanderers and Oxford University had to be played in the morning because the players wanted to watch the Boat Race in the afternoon.

Arsenal did not win their first major trophy until 1930 when they finally secured the FA Cup by beating Huddersfield 2–0. However, the game will probably be remembered for the German airship, the Graf Zeppelin, dipping low over Wembley during the course of the match to give the passengers a bird's-eye view.

In the 1898/99 season Glasgow Rangers won all eighteen of their games, scoring seventy-nine goals and conceding eighteen.

Jimmy Lindsay, who began his career with West Ham in 1966, was born on 12 July 1949.

In the 1959/60 season Derek Reeves of Southampton scored the greatest number of goals recorded in a Division II season, thirty-nine.

Bert Trautman, the Manchester City goalkeeper, broke his neck during the 1956 FA Cup final and was voted Footballer of the Year.

When West Ham won the European Cup-winners' Cup in 1965 they were watched by a crowd of 100,000, a record for the competition.

The **World Cup competition was instituted in Montevideo, Uruguay, on 13 July 1930.**

Major Mandarin, who played for the Royal Engineers in their first two FA Cup finals, was referee in the following eight finals.

Just after Derby County had won Division I in 1972, Brian Clough was in his office dictating letters to a temporary secretary who had only arrived that morning. He asked her to append his name to one letter, to which she answered after a pause, 'And who are you?'

After playing for Liverpool in every round of the FA Cup competition in 1950, Bob Paisley was left out of the side that played in the final.

The first match played in the first World Cup competition resulted in a 4–1 victory for France over Mexico, with Laurent scoring the first World Cup goal. French national pride was heightened since news of the victory coincided with Bastille Day, 14 July.

In the 1879 quarter-final between Darwin and a team of Old Etonians Darwin scored four times in the final quarter of an hour to level the score at 5–5, and also included in the side the first two professional footballers ever seen in London.

Hugo Meisel, the manager of the Austrian Wunderteam of the 1934 World Cup, said after the final which they lost 0–1 to Italy that they would have won the cup if they could have had the English player Cliff Bastin in their side.

Just 200 yards separates the grounds of Dundee and Dundee United.

During **England's 1966 World Cup match against France on 15 July Nobby Stiles fouled Jacky Simon in front of the Royal Box and a number of England officials suggested that Alf Ramsey should drop him from the side. 'If he goes, I go', said Ramsey — and they both stayed.**

In 1975 only 4,963 people turned up to see Millwall play against Notts County. The principal reason, apart from the bad weather on the day, was a hoax telephone call saying that the match had been postponed which led to notices being put up at local railway stations.

In 1979 Alan Ball became the first player to make 100 appearances for four separate Football League clubs: Blackpool, Everton, Arsenal and Southampton.

The greatest crowd ever to watch a football match flocked to the Brazil-Uruguay World Cup match in Rio de Janeiro on 16 July 1950, filling the stadium with 205,000 people.

Brazil were so confident that they would win the World Cup in 1950 that a special victory song had already been composed. When they lost 1–2 to Uruguay, the song was never heard again.

Not one member of the Bolton team that won the FA Cup in 1958 had cost the club more than his £10 signing-on fee.

In 1950 a number of leading British football players were involved in an attempt by South American clubs to lure them with offers of £4,000 signing fees and wages of £100 a month.

On 17 July 1920 England recorded their largest victory over South Africa in a football test when they beat the home team 9–1 in Cape Town.

M.P. Betts, who scored in the first FA Cup final, played under the assumed name of A.H. Chequer, which he took from the Old Harrovian side the Harrow Chequers.

King's Park's Alex Haddon scored hat-tricks in five consecutive Scottish Division II matches in 1932 with four goals against Armadale, five against Stenhousemuir and three against Edinburgh City, Montrose and Brechin City.

The Italian League team that drew with the Scottish League at Hampden Park in 1961 contained Messrs. Law, Charles and Hitchins.

John Richie, who came on as a substitute for Stoke City in their match with Kaiserslautern in the 1972 UEFA Cup match and was sent off forty seconds later, was born on 18 July 1941.

As a teenager Rose Reilly was a real life *Gregory's Girl*, although she played for a Scottish boys' team without it being realized in what respect she differed from her team mates. As a mature female player she represented Stewarton Thistle, and the former Scottish team manager, Ally McLeod once admitted, 'If she was a boy, I wouldn't have any hesitation at all in signing her. She has remarkable talent.'

In 1972 Dixie Deans scored only the second hat-trick in a Scottish Cup final when he played for Celtic against Hibs. The first had come sixty-eight years earlier when Jimmy Quinn also scored for Celtic.

Rafael Villazan, who was born on 19 July 1956, became the first Uruguayan player to play in the Football League when he signed for Wolves in 1980.

The 1877 Cup final was the first to run into extra time when the Wanderers beat Oxford University.

Don Rogers, responsible for Swindon Town's revival in the late 1960s, was compared with an earlier hero, Harold Fleming. A dazzling inside-forward, Fleming was capped eleven times for England between 1909 and 1914. He held deep religious convictions and refused to play football on Good Friday or Christmas Day. When Swindon reached the League Cup final in 1969, Fleming's statue was decorated with a single red and white rosette.

In 1968 Barrow were near the top of Division III. Four years later they failed to be re-elected to the Football League.

The meeting of the Football Association held on 20 July 1871 recorded this proposal, 'That it is desirable that a Challenge Cup should be established in connection with the Association, for which all clubs belonging to the Association should be invited to compete.' This proposal was finally approved in October that year and so the FA Cup competition came into being.

The first FA Cup final to be replayed was when the Royal Engineers beat the Old Etonians 2-0 after an 1875 1-1 draw.

Crewe Alexandra achieved both their record attendance and their record defeat (2-13) in their FA Cup replay with Spurs in 1960.

In 1903 Bury won the FA Cup without conceding a goal. The only other team to achieve this was the Preston North End side that won the double in 1889.

Three weeks after their record win against a national side (17–0) England played their final Test against Australia in their 1951 tour and won 5–0 on 21 July. Their aggregate for the tour was thirty-two goals and they conceded two.

The Milk Cup was the brainchild of the former League secretary Alan Hardaker. The first Milk Cup goal was scored by Maurice Cook of Fulham during their 1–2 defeat by Bristol Rovers.

Bill Perry, who scored the winning goal in the famous Matthews FA Cup final of 1953, was the last South African player to win an FA Cup winners' medal.

Raith Rovers are the only British League club side to fail to win a home match. In the 1962/63 season they lost fifteen games and drew two.

22 July is the birthday of Ron Springett, one of the leading British goalkeepers of the late 1950s and 60s, who made his first England appearance in November 1959 and played in goal in all but one of the next twenty-nine internationals. In the 1967/68 season he conceded only thirty-six goals when playing for Queen's Park Rangers — the lowest in the league.

In 1958 Stan Crowther was allowed to play for Manchester United in the FA Cup, in spite of having played for Aston Villa in an earlier round. The Football League allowed this because of the Munich air disaster. Manchester reached the final but lost 0–2 to Bolton. The year before Crowther had been a member of the Aston Villa side that had also beaten Manchester United in the final.

In the 1920s Raith Rovers were shipwrecked while on a tour of the Canary Islands.

The match between England and Argentina on 23 July 1966 in the World Cup competition was held up by seven minutes while the Argentinian captain, Rattin, argued with the referee and refused to be sent off, before finally leaving the pitch.

In 1948 Manchester United won the FA Cup without playing one tie at Old Trafford. They had three home draws, but they were played at Maine Road, which they were sharing with Manchester City at the time.

Alun Evans, who scored a hat-trick for Liverpool in their European Fairs Cup match with Bayern Munich in the 1970/71 season, was the first Liverpool player to score three goals in a European match and his transfer fee from Wolves made him the first £100,000 teenage player in British football.

Kerry Dixon's birthday.

When the post of manager fell vacant at Watford in July 1971 one of the first applicants was twelve-year-old Julia Padek. The appointment was finally given to George Kibby.

Crewe Alexandra's ground at Gresty Road was the setting for two FA Cup semi-finals in the 1880s.

The French magazine *L'Equipe* once commented, 'If the French were as good at playing football as they are thinking about it, then the next World Cup would be a foregone conclusion.'

England and Australia played the final test of the first England tour on 25 July 1925. The tourists had scored a total of twenty-two goals from five tests against the host nation's three.

In reaching the 1970 FA Cup final Chelsea scored fifteen of their twenty-one goals in the competition during the last half of the draw.

During a Scottish Southern League match in 1945 Kilmarnock were ordered to take the same penalty seven times against Partick Thistle and eventually missed it.

When Newcastle became Division I champions in 1907 they lost in the first round of the FA Cup to Crystal Palace, who were then the bottom club in the Southern League.

The Charlton brothers scored all three goals in England's World Cup semi-final win over Portugal on 26 July 1966. Bobby scored England's two and Jack gave away the penalty that allowed Portugal to kick their one goal.

Tranmere Rover's Welsh international goalkeeper Bert Gray won the professional footballer golf championship three times.

Only Billy Liddell of Liverpool and Stanley Matthews played in Great Britain's sides that took on the Rest of Europe in 1947 and 1955.

When Geoff Hurst joined Stoke City in July 1973 he was asked for reasons by one interviewer and replied, 'Firstly I won't have to play against Denis Smith. Secondly so I don't have to take penalties against Gordon Banks.'

27

Professionalism was legalized by the Football Association in July 1885.

The former Derby goalkeeper Ray Middleton played non-League football for Boston United in the early 1950s and was playing in goal for Boston when they went to Derby's Baseball Ground and beat the home side 6–1.

Between 1927 and 1930 Hartlepool United was eliminated from the FA Cup competition by non-League sides.

Mandel Francisco Dos Santos, better known as Carrincha, got his nickname meaning 'little bird' from his pursuit of 'little birds'.

28

28 July is the birthday of Duncan Welbourne, who as a player with Watford played in every one of their matches throughout five consecutive seasons.

In spite of Billy Minter scoring six goals for St Albans in their FA Cup fourth-round replay against Dulwich Hamlet in 1922 they still lost the match 7–8.

Cardiff City, the FA Cup winners in 1927, were bottom of Division III (North) in 1933/34.

At the turn of the century a football supplier in Liverpool was advertising the following items: 'Footballs 9/6 (round, sound and durable); Knickers (wide fitting but not baggy) 1/6, 1/11, 2/6, 3/6; Shirts (well sewn and comfortable) 2/3, 2/9, 3/6; Boots (with permanent toes, on good lasts, easy yet tight fitting) 10/6; Shin guards 10d, 1/6, 2/6; Goal nets 30/-, 35/-, 48/-.'

Alvin Martin, who began his career with West Ham in July 1976, was born on 29 July 1958.

The FA Cup semi-final between Sheffield United and Liverpool went to four matches before Sheffield won 1-0. The first game ended in a 2-2 draw, the second in a 1-1 draw and the third was abandoned when Liverpool were leading 1-0. Sheffield reversed that score on their fourth and final meeting. This was the first time that an FA Cup match proper had to go to four games.

Charles Foweraker joined Bolton Wanderers as part-time gate checker in 1895 and stayed with the club for fifty years, serving in various capacities. He was the secretary-manager during their three Cup final victories at Wembley between 1923 and 1929.

Stanley Matthews' father was a boxer known as the 'fighting barber of Hanley'.

When England beat West Germany 4-2 to win the World Cup on 30 July 1966 Geoff Hurst's three goals became the highest total scored by a single player in any World Cup final.

Between 1910 and 1930 James Gordon of Rangers played in every position for the club.

The attendance at Highland League matches in Scotland is often greater than that for Scottish League Division II games.

When two points were awarded for a win and one for a draw, Doncaster Rovers set a record in the 1946/47 seaon with seventy-two points. In the 1904/05 season they set a record at the other extreme with a Division II points total of eight!

Between 1910 and 1930 James Gordon of Rangers played in every position for the club.

Cameron Buchanan of Wolves, who had been born on 31 July 1928, made his Football League debut a mere fourteen years later in a wartime League match in 1942.

Herbert Barrow scored the first goal in the 1939 FA Cup final for Portsmouth in their 4–1 victory over Wolves, just two months after joining Portsmouth from Wolves.

Manchester United were the first club to lose successive FA Cup finals at Wembley when they were beaten in 1958. Only Bobby Charlton and Bill Foulkes played in both finals.

When England toured Australia in 1952 the Football Association put up a trophy then valued at £500 for a competition among the states. However, there was little enthusiasm for this competition in a country where rugby league and Australian rules football had loyal followings.

Kick-off

The season starts in August, and that first game is critical in establishing a team's confidence. There have been practice matches, of course, often against clubs from lower leagues, and these can often produce some unexpected defeats. But it seems to me that the worse the record in the practice games, the better a club performs when it comes to the real thing. Getting a goal in the first five minutes of the first match of the season can be worth two months of pre-season training; going one down can have the reverse effect.

One opening match that will always stick in mind was a home fixture Fulham had with Blackburn Rovers. Bedford Jezzard, then the England centre-forward as well as Fulham's, got stuck in the traffic on Putney Bridge. He tried to squeeze past the other cars on the inside, and he so annoyed another driver that this man began shaking his fist at him — with the result that he drove slap into the back of the car in front. Beddie burst out laughing and couldn't wait to tell us about it. However, he panted into the dressing-room only ten minutes before kick-off, by which time Frank Osborne had told Tony Barton, the twelfth man in the team, to get ready for the game.

'Where have you been?' Frank asked Beddie, to which he replied, 'I got held up.'

'Well, you're not playing,' Frank told him.

'Who's not playing?' asked Beddie.

'Oh ... all right,' Frank said. 'Get your kit on.'

We beat Blackburn 5-0 that afternoon, and Beddie scored three of the goals! He really didn't have time to tell us about the smash on the bridge until after the game was over.

August

The very first European Cup-winners' Cup match was played on 1 August 1960 in Berlin between ASK Vorwaerts and Red Star Brno.

Everton scored 121 goals in the 1931/32 season and in one match at the Valley all five Everton forwards scored within eighteen minutes.

On his Scottish League debut in 1930 Jimmy Dyet scored eight goals for King's Park in their match against Forfar Athletic in a Scottish League Division II game.

When Norman Whiteside played for Northern Ireland in the 1982 World Cup he became the youngest player to represent his country in the competition. He was seventeen years forty-two days old at the time, beating Pele's record by 195 days.

The longest game of football played at first-class level started at 9.30 pm on 2 August 1962 in the Copa Libertadores in Santos Brazil, between Santos and the Uruguayan club Penarol FC. With interruptions, the game lasted three and a half hours until 1.00 am the following morning and resulted in a 3–3 draw.

Genoa, founded in 1893, are the oldest Italian Football League club.

A total of around £11,900,000 was paid for the Argentinian player Diego Maradona in two transfers in 1982 and 1984.

The Rio de Janeiro club, Fluminese, was founded in 1902 with an Englishman, Oscar Cox, as its first president.

3

Jimmy Greenhoff was transferred during the European Fairs' Cup final of August 1968. Having played the first leg for Leeds United against Ferencvaros, he had moved to Birmingham City by the time of the second leg.

In August 1975 Dave Sexton's Queen's Park Rangers beat three different League champions. They had a 4–1 win over West German Bundesliga champions Moenchengladbach; a 4–2 victory over the Portuguese champions Benfica; and in the first week of the Football League fixtures they beat Derby County 5–1. They finished that season one point short of the League champions, Liverpool.

In 1957 John Charles became the first British player to be transferred to a foreign club, when he moved to Juventus from Leeds for £65,000.

4

On 4 August 1938 Arsenal paid Wolves £14,000 for Bryn Jones which stood as a British transfer record until 1947.

In 1966 Alan Ball became the first player to be transferred between English clubs for £100,000 when he moved from Blackpool to Everton.

Sam Bartram kept goal in four consecutive Wembley finals: two wartime South Cup finals and two FA Cup finals.

The FA Challenge Trophy grew out of an FA decision in 1969 to organize a competition for semi-professional clubs. The first winners in 1970 were Macclesfield Town who beat Telford 2–0.

The first time that penalty kicks were used as a tie-breaker in a first-class match in England was on 5 August 1970 in a semi-final of the Watney Cup between Hull City and Manchester United. After a 1-1 tie at the end of extra time, Manchester United won 4-3 on penalties.

Peterborough's first season in the Football League, 1960/61, is one they will long remember. They ended the season Division IV champions having won twenty-eight matches, scored 134 goals and amassed sixty-six points. Terry Bly was top goalscorer with fifty-two goals.

The FA Vase replaced the Amateur Cup in 1975. Its first winners were Hoddesdon Town who beat Epsom 2-1.

Dixie Dean played for Sligo Rovers in the 1939 FA of Ireland Cup final which they lost 1-0 to Shelborne after a 1-1 draw.

Kevin Keegan was sent off twice in five days in August 1974. The first occasion was in a match against Kaiserslautern, followed soon after by the Charity Shield match in which he was joined by Billy Bremner from Liverpool's opposition, Leeds United.

Half-way through the 1973/74 season Alex Stepney, Manchester United's goalkeeper, was the side's leading goal-scorer with two penalties.

In 1953 Falkirk became the first Scottish side to tour Malta.

When L. Sanon of Haiti scored against Italy in the first match of the 1974 World Cup competition, he brought to an end Dino Zoff's run of eleven matches without conceding a goal for Italy.

Two great World Cup players, Gordon Banks and Tostao, both announced their retirement on 7 August 1973 and both left the game because of eye injuries.

S. Milton made his debut for Halifax Town in a match against Stockport County in 1934 and let in thirteen goals.

Cape Town-born Eddie Firmani was a very travelled player. After five seasons with Charlton until 1955, he joined the Italian League club Sampdoria and later moved to Inter Milan and Genoa. He was capped for Italy on three occasions in 1963 before returning to Charlton. In May 1965 he went to Southend and three years later began his third stay at the Valley.

Frank Clark won a League Cup winners' medal with Nottingham Forest in 1978 after helping Crook Town to win the Amateur Cup sixteen years earlier.

Misfortune dogged East Stirling on 8 August 1981 as they battled to make their way to their Scottish League Cup tie with Montrose. No fewer than three coaches broke down on the way to the game and the journey had to be completed by taxi. Then having arrived they were beaten 1–0.

In the 1957/58 season Manchester City scored 104 goals and conceded 100, making them the only club with goals both for and against that ran to three figures in a single season.

Port Vale's left-half, Alan Hardaker, is the only professional footballer since 1945 who was a parson.

Northern Ireland's manager, Billy Bingham, was once manager of Greece.

_____ **9** _____

Mario Zagalo, the only man who has both won a World Cup winners' medal and managed a World Cup winning team (Brazil), was born on 9 August 1931.

This day is also the birthday of the former Wolves player, Chris Dangerfield, who played for five different sides in the North American Soccer League in the five seasons between 1975 and 1979: Portland Timbers, Las Vegas Quicksilver, Team Hawaii, California Surf and Los Angeles Aztecs.

The first Professional Footballers' Association awards were given in 1974. Norman Hunter was Player of the Year and Kevin Beattie Young Player of the Year.

Only St Mirren achieved success for Scotland in the Anglo-Scottish Cup between 1976 and 1981.

_____ **10** _____

Starting on 10 August 1968, Michael Jones and Bob Wilson of Shrewsbury viewed League matches in all ninety-three Football League grounds in England, including that of Berwick Rangers. They completed the sequence 264 days later on 30 April 1969.

J.C. Burns made 263 appearances for Queen's Park Rangers and Brentford while he was still amateur.

Only two players, Peppino Mezza and Giovanni Ferrari, survived from the Italian World Cup-winning team of 1934 to retain the cup four years later.

In 1920 Spurs became the first reserve club to win the Football Combination.

''Ere, skip, I think you'll find it's the football *combination we've won!*'

Steve Murray was appointed manager of Forfar Athletic in August 1980 and resigned from the post three days later.

The 100th FA Cup Final in 1981 was also the first occasion when a Cup final was replayed at Wembley.

In a Scottish Ladies League match played in 1975 Edinburgh Dynamos Football Club beat Lochend Thistle 42–0.

Sheffield Wednesday reached the 1890 FA Cup final after negotiating a problematic quarter-final with Notts County. At their first meeting, which Sheffield won 5–0, Notts complained about the pitch and the game was replayed. This time Notts won 3–2, but it was Sheffield's turn to make a protest, this time about an ineligible player fielded by Notts. So the tie went to a third game which passed without incident and saw Sheffield win by two goals to one.

Pat Jennings scored for Spurs from his own goal area during the Charity Shield match they played against Manchester United on 12 August 1967.

Dick Harbin played in 48 Football League matches in the 1974/75 season: twenty-seven times for Reading before being transferred to Rotherham where he played twenty-one times.

When Wimbledon beat Sutton United 4–2 to win the 1963 Amateur Cup, Eddie Reynolds scored all four goals with his head.

Kilmarnock played with seven players in their 1–4 defeat by Port Glasgow Rangers in 1908: the other four failed to turn up.

The first player to be sent off at Wembley was Boris Stankovic of Yugoslavia during the Olympic Games football final on 13 August 1948 against Sweden.

Stanley Davies, who won eighteen international caps for Wales between 1920 and 1930 played in six different positions: right-half (twice), left-half (once), outside-right (twice), inside-right (three times), centre-forward (six times) and inside-left (four times).

In the 1972/73 season Michael Jones scored 294 goals in sixty-seven games for Afan Lido FC, St Joseph's School and Port Talbot Boys XI: sixty-five headers; 120 from the right foot; and 109 from the left foot. This included one score of eleven goals, one of ten and six triple hat-tricks.

On 13 August 1966 Archie Gemmell became the first substitute to come on in a Scottish first-class match when he was called on by St Mirren against Clyde.

Barnsley lost 1–2 to Lincoln in the first leg of their first-round League Cup tie. When they met for the second leg on 14 August it was Lincoln's turn to be defeated by the same margin after extra time, when Barnsley made good use of the recently introduced penalty shoot-out to win 4–3 on penalties.

In spite of being the leading goal-scorer in Division I with twenty-one goals, Mick Channon still was not able to save his club Southampton from relegation in the 1973/74 season. The same fate befell Bob Hatton of Blackpool four years later when he was leading goal-scorer in Division II with twenty-two goals.

Bohemians of Dublin are the only one of the founding members still in the League of Ireland.

On 15 August 1981 New Zealand beat Fiji 13–0 to record the highest score in any World Cup qualifying match.

Andy Wilson was leading goal-scorer for two clubs in the 1923/24 season with a total of only thirteen goals: eight for Middlesbrough and five for Chelsea.

The 1933/34 Welsh Cup was contested between Bristol City and Tranmere Rovers at Chester, with Bristol winning 3–0. In fact the Welsh Cup did not return to Wales until 1948.

Scunthorpe conceded only nine goals in their twenty-three home matches in their first Football League season, 1950/51.

Peter Farrell, the player who scored the winning goal when the Republic of Ireland claimed their one victory over England in 1949, was born on 16 August 1922. Although normally positioned at wing-half, he scored the crucial goal as an inside-right.

Aston Villa's full-back Peter Aldis headed a goal from thirty-five yards in a match against Sunderland in 1952.

Dave Esson scored forty-five goals for Arbroath in the 1958/59 season when no other player in the side reached double figures.

In 1950/51 Birmingham Synthonia did not concede a single goal in their Northern League programme.

In August 1898 Glasgow Rangers began a winning run in the Scottish League Division I which saw them win all eighteen of their league matches in the 1898/99 season and the first four in the following season.

In 1927 West Bromwich Albion's Jimmy Cookson scored the fastest 100 Football League goals when he took his tally to a century in his eighty-seventh match.

The 1938 World Cup first-round match between Brazil and Poland resulted in a thrilling 6–5 win for Brazil in extra time. This was the only occasion in the history of the World Cup when individual players from each side have scored four goals in a match, Wilimonski for Poland and Leonardis for Brazil.

In the 1959/60 season Joe Baker (Hibernian) became the first professional footballer to play for England when not playing for a Football League club.

Just Fontaine, the record World Cup goal-scorer with thirteen goals for France from six games in the 1958 finals in Sweden, was born in Marrakesh on 18 August 1933.

In spite of scoring a record number of goals in a season (1930/31) Aston Villa still finished the season runners-up, seven points behind Arsenal. Their total of 128 included twenty games when they scored four or more goals.

The 1985 Football League Cup final might have brought back memories for Asa Hartford when playing for Norwich against Sunderland. Sixteen years earlier he had been sent off in the Youth FA Cup final when playing for West Brom, and his opponents on that occasion had also been Sunderland.

The FA Youth Cup was first held in 1953 and was won by Manchester United who took the cup in its first five years.

Until they lost to Everton in August 1969, Leeds United had gone for thirty-four Division I matches without loss; their previous defeat had been to Burnley the October before.

The first man to be transferred between Scottish clubs for a fee of over £100,000 was Colin Stein, who moved to Rangers from Hibs in 1969.

Manchester United scratched in the first round of the 1959 European Cup and the Swiss Team, Young Boys Berne, won on a walkover and reached the semi-finals.

The Spanish League had an influx of foreign players in the late 1950s, among them Di Stefano (Argentina); Puskas Kocsis, Czibor and Kubala (Hungary); Di Di (Brazil); and Santamaria (Uruguay). In fact in 1959 there were sixty foreign players in the Spanish League.

Eleven years before joining Liverpool, Kenny Dalglish had played for Liverpool's 'B' team against Southport on 20 August 1966, while spending a two-week trial period with the club, before returning to Celtic.

Between 1974 and 1979 Peter Noble scored from twenty-seven consecutive penalties for Burnley.

1950 was the only time when the World Cup final was decided by a league table that looked like this:

Uruguay 2	Spain 2	Brazil 7	Sweden 1
Uruguay 3	Sweden 2	Brazil 6	Spain 1
Sweden 3	Spain 1	Uruguay 2	Brazil 1

So Uruguay won with five points, followed by Brazil with four, Sweden with two and Spain with one. (Ghiggia scored in all of Uruguay's matches.)

21

Keith Peacock became the first substitute to be used in a Football League match when he went on for Charlton Athletic in their match with Bolton Wanderers on 21 August 1965. On the same afternoon Bobby Knox of Barrow became the first substitute to score in a Football League match when he kicked a goal against Wrexham.

Cardifff once had the best defensive record in Division I, conceding only fifty-nine goals, but this did not prevent their relegation.

The Uruguayan national team have the nickname 'Celestos' because of their sky-blue shirts.

Peter Terson's play *Zigger Zagger* takes its title from the chant of the avid Stoke fan, J. Bageley.

22

The first *Match of the Day* was shown on 22 August 1964 when Liverpool beat Arsenal 3–2 at Anfield.

Ralph Banks was playing left-back for Bolton when they lost the 1953 FA Cup final to Blackpool. His brother Tom fared better five years later when, playing in the same position for Bolton, they won the cup.

In 1899 Frank and Fred Forman became the first pair of brothers to play for England in the same match, while attached to the same Football League club (Nottingham Forest).

Sunderland's Derek Foster became the youngest player to play in Division I, when at the age of fifteen years and 185 days he was picked for the game against Leicester on 22 August 1964.

Brighton played their first Division II match on 23 August 1958 and lost 0–9 to Middlesbrough.

Since their formation in 1866 Chesterfield have played at the same ground.

The England forward line that faced Scotland in 1937 had three players from Stoke City: Matthews, Steel and Johnson.

Cento of Real Madrid has played in a record six European Cup winning teams: 1956, 1957, 1958, 1959, 1960 and 1966.

On 24 August 1968 the main stand at Nottingham Forest's ground caught fire and the police had to evacuate 34,000 spectators.

Bristol Rovers' ground at Eastville is the smallest Football League ground.

The Czechoslovak player Ondrus scored a goal for both sides in the 1976 European Nations Cup semi-final.

Two players died during the Army Cup final of 1948 in the presence of the King and Queen.

'How are we going to get another twenty players on to this pitch?'

On **25 August 1928 Rotherham lost 1–11 to Bradford City, the first of two defeats that season in which ten or more goals were scored against them. The second was inflicted by South Shields who beat them 10–1 on 16 March 1929.**

West Ham fielded three goalkeepers in their match against Lincoln City in 1948: Ernie Gregory, Tom Moroney and George Dick. They lost 3–4 and Lincoln's Jack Dodds scored against all three.

In the 1958 FA Youth Cup final Wolves beat Chelsea 7–6 on aggregate after losing the first leg 1–5.

Two Watford players, C. Holton and E. Uphill, were top goal-scorers in Division IV in the 1959/60 season with forty-two and thirty goals respectively.

Discussions took place between Clyde and Hamilton Academical in August 1970 with the idea of the two clubs sharing Douglas Park (Hamilton's home ground) for their home games. The idea met with strong opposition from Hamilton which closed the matter.

Birmingham City's goalkeeper Tony Coton did not have to wait long to get a touch of the ball in the Football League. Eighty seconds after the kick off in his first match against Sunderland in 1980, Coton faced a penalty and saved it.

The Italian side Fiorentina had a run of thirty-three League matches without a defeat.

Paraguay were among the countries that competed in the 1958 World Cup finals.

Derek Reeves, holder of the Division III post-1945 scoring record with thirty-nine goals from forty-six games and joint holder of the highest individual score (five goals) in a Football League Cup tie, was born on 27 August 1934.

Grimsby's goalkeeper Walter Scott saved three penalties in their match against Burnley in 1909.

Crewe Alexandra have never reached an FA Cup final in spite of being one of the original members of the Football League. However, two of their former players have refereed in the finals: Arthur Scragg in 1899 and Jackie Pearson in 1911.

The Italian team Juventus are known as *La Vecchia Signora* which means 'the grand old lady'.

'That's Juliano from Juventus — he's known as the grand old man.'

Swindon Town celebrated their League debut on 28 August 1920 with a 9-1 Division III (South) victory against Luton Town.

Emlyn Hughes, who celebrates his birthday on this day, played in seventy-four first-class matches for Liverpool in the 1972/73 season: forty-one Division I, four FA Cup, eight League Cup, twelve UEFA Cup and twelve full international games and the Common Market match of the Three against the Six.

The 1952 Newcastle United team fielded players who had represented five different countries: Jackie Milburn (England); Bobby Mitchell and Frank Brennan (Scotland); Billy Foulkes (Wales); Alf McMichael (Northern Ireland); and George Robledo (Chile).

All eleven players picked for the England team to play Wales in 1894 and 1895 came from the Corinthians.

Everton beat Wimbledon in the second round of the League Cup with a score of 8-0 on 29 August 1978.

Between the 1933/34 and 1936/37 seasons Charlton Athletic rose from being fifth in Division III (South) to runners-up in Division I.

A junior game between Bridgeport and Collin Green in Lisburn, Northern Ireland, had to be abandoned after both teams, the referee and the linesman had turned up to find that somebody had forgotten to provide the goal-posts!

In 1946 Dr Kevin O'Flanagan represented Northern Ireland against Scotland and Wales, playing football against the Scots and rugby against the Welsh.

Emlyn Hughes's birthday is 28 August.

The **Dutch footballer Marc de Clerck made a sensational first team debut for Aberdeen on 30 August 1980 as cover for the usual Aberdeen goalkeeper, Bobby Clark. Twenty-two minutes into the match de Clerck made a drop goal clearance which was missed by Berwick Rangers centre-half and their goalkeeper on its way into the Berwick net.**

In the eight years from 1961 to 1969 Northampton Town rose from Division IV to Division I and slid back to Division IV once again.

From making his debut for Celtic on 30 August 1980 in which he came on as a substitute against Stirling Albion and scored twice, Charlie Nicholas went on to score a further nine goals in his next seven matches.

The first day on which a full League fixture list was played after the end of the Second World War was 31 August 1946. The last occasion had been the day before war was declared, 2 September 1939.

In the closing weeks of the 1957/58 season Lincoln City were lying at the bottom of Division II with six games to play. Within a period of eighteen days they managed to win all six games and so avoided relegation by one point.

It was a case of third time lucky for the Yugoslav defender Velibor Vasovic when he played in the European Cup final in 1970. In 1966 he had headed the first goal for Partizan Belgrade in a match they eventually lost to Real Madrid 1–2. In 1969 he scored from the penalty spot for Ajax but they lost 1–4 to AC Milan. Finally in 1970 he captained Ajax to beat the Greek side Panathinaikos 2–0.

Kick-off

If there is one perfect month in the year for playing football, it is probably September. The weather is starting to get cooler, and the grass is in the best condition it will be in all season. The ground is starting to soften up without being muddy and sticky. Nowadays, artificial grass — which the National Playing Fields Association also uses to advantage on occasion — has been developed by quite a few manufacturers to produce surfaces that give exactly the same bounce and play as well in every respect, as natural grass does. The ball will not slow up or speed up on artificial grass any more that it will on the real thing, and the structure of the layers beneath the surface is such that there is just a little give that will go with a foot turn and provide adequate cushioning when you fall.

I would hate to see natural grass pitches replaced entirely, but in the right circumstances — like those selected by the charity — the new artificial surfaces are a wonderful bonus that deserve to be used whenever they are practical and desirable.

Until the 1914/15 season the opening day of the Football League season was always 1 September, unless it was a Friday or a Sunday.

The great German player and national team manager Helmut Schon was born on 1 September 1915.

The Yorkshire cricketer, David Bairstow, who celebrates his birthday on this date, played League football for Bradford City in the 1971/72 season.

The greatest aggregate victory ever recorded by a British club was the 21–0 European Cup-winners' Cup victory by Chelsea over Jeunesse Hautcharace of Luxembourg in September 1971. The first leg resulted in an 8–0 away win, followed by a 13–0 win in the second leg played at Stamford Bridge, in which Peter Osgood scored five goals.

September

2

The lowest single attendance for a League Cup match was 1,737 when Lincoln City faced Bradford PA in a first-round tie in September 1961.

During the 1953/54 season Port Vale did not concede a goal in thirty of their forty-six Division III (North) matches.

When the Swedish club Malmo reached the 1979 European Cup final their manager was the former Fulham player Bobby Houghton.

In 1962 Va Va of Brazil became the first player to score in successive World Cup finals.

3

Jimmy Delaney, born on 3 September 1914, nearly achieved the unique record of earning winners' medals in four national football association cup finals. In 1937 he won a Scottish Cup winners' medal with Celtic, with Manchester United in 1948 he won an FA Cup winners' medal and he was with Derry City in 1954 when they won the Irish Cup. But two years later Shamrock Rovers came runners-up to Cork Athletic in the FA of Ireland Cup final, depriving him of his fourth winners' medal.

J. Saldumnere of the Argentinian club Racing-Mar-Del-Plata made 412 consecutive appearances and then broke his leg.

The Republic of Ireland recorded their biggest defeat in 1982 when they were beaten 0–7 by Brazil in Belo Horizonte.

Tony Book, born on 4 September 1935, who was joint footballer of the year in 1969 with Dave Mackay, did not make his Football League debut until he was in his thirtieth year.

Between 1972 and 1979 Stan Bowles made thirty-four transfer requests during his stay at Queen's Park Rangers.

Seven goals were scored during a match between Blackburn Rovers and Liverpool in Division I in 1896, but only one of them was credited. Blackburn won 1–0.

The French League club Monaco received a boost for the 1980/81 season when their best known patron, Prince Rainier, ordered shirts in Scotland's distinctive dark blue.

On 5 September 1885 Arbroath beat Bon Accord 36–0 to score the highest total in any British football match in a senior league. On the same day in the same competition (Scottish FA Cup) Dundee Harps beat Aberdeen Rovers 35–0.

On 5 September 1931 the Celtic goalkeeper, John Thomson, whom many regarded as the finest ever to play in Scotland, fractured his skull diving at the feet of the Rangers forward Sam English. He died of his injuries and 30,000 mourners attended his funeral.

Portsmouth, the Division I champions in 1950, are the only League champions since the Second World War to lose twice to two different teams: Blackpool and West Bromwich Albion.

By winning the 1966/67 European Fairs Cup final on 6 September, Dynamo Zagreb of Yugoslavia became the first eastern European country to win a major European competition.

On 6 September 1962 Dundee United won their very first European Cup match when they beat FC Cologne 8–1.

Port Vale reached the fifth round of the FA Cup in the 1885/86 season without playing a match.

Chelsea's Irish international inside-forward of the 1930s, Tom Priestley, always wore a rugby scrum cap when he played. He had lost all his hair through illness as a child.

Geoff Vowden of Birmingham became the first substitute in the Football League to score a hat-trick on 7 September 1968.

Liverpool reached their first European Cup semi-final in 1964/65 on the toss of a coin after playing three drawn games against FC Cologne.

The former Rangers centre-half J. Simpson is the father of Celtic's Ronnie Simpson who has played in an FA Cup final, a European Cup final, in addition to every major Scottish final, as well as representing Great Britain in the Olympic Games football tournament.

When Helmut Schon became West Germany's team manager in 1964 there had only been two others before him: Otto Nerz from 1926 to 1936 and Sepp Hereberger from then until 1964.

George Cox of Aston Villa scored the first own goal (for Wolves) on the first day of the first Football League competition, 8 September 1888.

Brian Clough failed to score in either of his England appearances, but in September 1959, a month before his internationals, he had scored five goals for the English League's match against the Irish League.

Before finalizing his World Cup team in 1966 Alf Ramsey had tried playing wingers in all the group matches. He reverted to the 4-3-3 format after Geoff Hurst joined the team for the quarter-final against Argentina.

Sheffield United's full-back Harry Trickett took to the field for the 1899 FA Cup final strapped with fifty yards of bandages to protect broken ribs and a ruptured side.

'Harry's overdone it with the bandages, don't you think?'

— ⑨ —

On 9 September 1916 second Lieutenant Donald Bell, formerly a Bradford Park Avenue full-back, became the only Football League player ever to win the VC. This was awarded posthumously 'for most conspicuous bravery' shown by him on the Somme.

On 9 September 1980 Eammon Collins of Blackpool became the youngest peace-time player to take part in a senior game involving a Football League club, when he appeared for Blackpool in an Anglo-Scottish Cup match against Kilmarnock. He was fourteen years 323 days old at the time.

The first North American Soccer League competition in 1967 was won by Oakland Clippers.

Aston Villa's Eric Houghton, who managed them to win the 1957 FA Cup, made his county cricket debut for Warwickshire in 1946, eighteen years after making his Football League debut for Aston Villa.

— ⑩ —

Sunderland played their first match at Roker Park on 10 September 1898 after it had been officially opened by the club president, the Marquis of Londonderry. They beat Liverpool 1–0 that afternoon. The following February their home ground was the setting for England's 8–2 win over Northern Ireland.

A few weeks before the 1954 World Cup finals began the German club Kaiserslautern lost 1–5 to Hanover in the German Cup final. In spite of this the German team manager Sepp Hereberger picked five Kaiserslautern players but none from Hanover. His selection proved sound and West Germany beat Hungary 3–2 to win the World Cup.

The first Scottish match shown live on television was the 1955 Scottish FA Cup final between Clyde and Celtic. The commentator was Ken Wolstenholme.

The FA Cup was stolen on the night of 11 September 1895 from the premises of a William Shillcock, a football outfitters in Newton Row, Birmingham. Sixty-eight years later a Sunday newspaper stated that an eighty-three-year-old man had confessed to having stolen the cup and melting it down to make half-crowns.

Birmingham City won Division II in 1948 by scoring more points than goals: 59 points to 55 goals.

In 1924 the Vale of Leven charged sixpence to enter for a Scottish League Division III match, rather than the requisite one shilling. The Scottish FA fined the club the difference between the two prices, now 2½ pence.

Ledger Ritson, playing full-back for Leyton Orient against Northampton on 11 September 1948, fractured his leg causing an injury that finally resulted in amputation two years later.

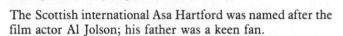

Leslie Compton, who was born on 12 September 1912, became England's oldest debutant in the home international championships when he was capped at the age of thirty-eight and two months.

The Scottish international Asa Hartford was named after the film actor Al Jolson; his father was a keen fan.

Both Norway and the Dutch East Indies played in their only World Cup finals in 1938. Norway lost 1–2 after extra time to the eventual winners, Italy, and the Dutch East Indies lost 0–6 to the other finalists Hungary.

Charlton Athletic's most capped player, John Hewie, played nineteen times for Scotland between 1956 and 1960, although he had been born in South Africa.

George Eastham senior, born on 13 September 1914, played alongside his son George as inside-forwards in the 1954/55 season for the Irish League club Ards.

The average attendance for Manchester United's home matches in 1967/68 was 57,549.

Alan Mullery had to miss England's 1964 tour of Brazil because he ricked his back while cleaning his teeth.

During the 1970 World Cup competition in Mexico Bobby Moore was accused of stealing a diamond bracelet. He was kept under indulgent house arrest for a few days before being allowed to join the rest of the party in Mexico City.

J. Heath of Wolves scored the first penalty in any Football League match, against Accrington on 14 September 1891.

Sheffield United, Huddersfield and Portsmouth are the only Division I champions who have also played in Division IV.

Lancashire clubs topped all four divisions in the Football League at the end of the 1972/73 season: Liverpool Division I, Burnley Division II, Bolton Division III and Southport Division IV.

Jerry and Joe Baker, brought up by Scottish parents, had unusual international careers. Joe played for England and Gerry emigrated and played for the USA.

When Aston Villa played the Turkish club Besiktas in the European Cup on 15 September 1982 there were no paying spectators to watch them win 3–1. This ban was the result of disciplinary action by UEFA.

In the decade between 1965 and 1975 Leeds United had a string of runner-up positions in major competitions: five in the League, three in the FA Cup, one in the European Cup and one in the European Fairs Cup. On the winning side they could count: two League championships, one FA Cup win and two European Fairs Cup victories.

The Chilean footballer Elias Figueroa was South American Footballer of the Year in 1974, 1975 and 1976.

Newport County's victory over Blackpool was embarrassing one season for their winger Kevin Moore. His father was President of Blackpool.

On 16 September 1922 John McIntyre scored four goals in five minutes for Blackburn Rovers in their match against Everton.

When Port Vale applied for re-election to the League, after suspension for some irregularities and unauthorized payments, their manager was Stanley Matthews and they were granted their re-instatement.

In the 1965/66 season Preston North End had sixteen Scottish-born players on their staff. In addition their manager Jimmy Milne was from Dundee, the team trainer Willie Cunningham had been born in Hill O'Beath and the club's chief scout was another Scotsman, appropriately named Jimmy Scott.

Germany's Gottfried Fuchs scored ten goals in their 16–0 win over Russia in 1912.

Nine different players scored in Liverpool's 11–0 victory over the Norwegian side Storomsgodset on 17 September 1974 in the first round of the European Cup-winners' Cup. Only Clemence and Hall failed to score.

Geoff Hurst was sent off for the first time in his career on 17 September 1972 while playing for Stoke City against Ipswich.

In 1888 Preston were clear favourites to win the FA Cup and insisted on having their picture taken with the cup before playing the final. The referee told them they had better win it first, and on the day West Brom beat them 2–1.

John Wark scored a record fourteen goals in Ipswich Town's UEFA Cup run in 1980/81.

Both Jim Milburn and Jack Froggatt of Leicester were credited with the same own goal in their Division I match against Chelsea on 18 September 1954. They both had the misfortune to touch the ball at the same time.

Peter Shilton was born on 18 September 1949.

The FA Sunday Cup was first held in 1965 when the winner was chosen on aggregate score and London beat Stafford.

The first European Super Cup was held in 1972 when Ajax beat Glasgow Rangers 6–3 on aggregate.

Peter Shilton was born on 18 September 1949.

On 19 September 1970 Mansfield House FC met Highfield FC reserves in the first round of the London FA Intermediate Cup. This ended in a draw and they had to meet on a further four occasions before Mansfield finally won a 2-0 victory. The total playing time for the tie was ten minutes under ten hours!

In the 1984/85 season Spurs won their first game at Anfield since 1912, but in the same season Bolton failed to win at Ashton Gate for the first time since 1907.

In 1950 The FA XI went on tour in Canada and played a match with the USA World Cup squad which they won 1-0 with a goal by Jimmy Hancock. On the boat on the way home news reached them of England's defeat by the USA in Belo Horizonte.

On 20 September 1947 Chris Marron scored ten goals for South Shields in their FA Cup preliminary game against Radcliffe.

Kevin Lock scored for both sides on two occasions in his career. The first was when he was playing for West Ham against Queen's Park Rangers in September 1977, and the second came two years later when he was playing for Fulham against Birmingham City.

Chesterfield reached the 1956 Youth Cup final, eventually losing to a Manchester United team that included players like Bobby Charlton, Wilf McGuinness, Albert Scanlon and Alex Dawson. Playing for Chesterfield that afternoon was another young player with a promising future: Gordon Banks.

When Newcastle won the 1969 European Fairs Cup they qualified the previous year by coming tenth in Division I.

England suffered their first home defeat by foreign opposition on 21 September 1949 when the Republic of Ireland beat them 2–0 at Goodison Park with goals by Martin and Farrell.

Cardiff City had seventeen internationals on their books in the 1925/26 season: nine Welsh, four Scottish and four Irish.

Fees for international appearances were doubled in 1887, rising from ten shillings to one pound.

In 1964 Morton fielded a goalkeeper named Mr X for a practice match. He naturally aroused a great deal of interest until the club signed him and his identity was revealed as Eric Sorensen of Denmark, the first Scandinavian footballer to make an impact on Scottish football.

On 22 September 1930 in the annual match between Sheffield and Glasgow, Sheffield were playing in white shirts with black shorts. The referee, J. Thompson, was dressed similarly and Sheffield's captain, Jimmy Seed, found himself passing to him in error. Realizing this, he asked the referee to put on a jacket. Mr Thompson agreed to be 'sent off' and the game renewed when he was more easily identifiable.

George Young of Rangers played in goal during the 1953 Scottish Cup final after the goalkeeper Niven had been injured. He was so successful that Rangers managed to force a replay against Aberdeen.

Between 1949 and 1969 Leicester City lost four Wembley FA Cup finals: to Wolves in 1949, to Spurs in 1961, to Manchester United in 1963 and to Manchester City in 1969.

Tom Finney came out of retirement on 23 September 1963 to play for Distillery in a European Cup match in Belfast.

Liverpool's Steve Heighway made his Republic of Ireland debut against Poland on 23 September 1970 before making his Football League debut.

Norway's international Thubjorn Svensson was the second player after Billy Wright to win 100 international caps.

Hartlepool's secretary-manager of the late 1920s and early 1930s, Bill Norman, set an example for his players one bitterly cold morning when they showed reluctance to strip for training. Seeing this, Norman stripped himself and rolled in the snow.

During his illustrious England career Nat Lofthouse scored thirty goals in internationals but never a hat-trick, although he did score two goals on ten occasions. However, on 24 September 1952 he scored six goals for the Football League against the League of Ireland.

Tinsley Lindley scored for England in eight consecutive internationals between 1886 and 1888.

The Yugoslav goalkeeper Dragon Pantelic scored three penalties in a league match for Radniki Nis against NK Zagreb in the 1980/81 season and himself saved a penalty.

In 1960 Bobby Charlton became the first footballer this century to score goals against Scotland in three successive matches. This had been achieved in the last century by E.C. Bambridge in 1879, 1880 and 1881 and by Tinsley Lindley in 1886, 1887 and 1888.

'Sorry, Bill, but the lads still won't strip!'

On 25 September 1983 Linda Curl scored twenty-two goals for Norwich Ladies in their 40–0 defeat of Milton Keynes reserves.

In the 1976/77 season Stan Bowles scored in the first five games that Queen's Park Rangers ever played in Europe.

Of the original twenty-two teams in Division III (South) in 1920 only one team, Merthyr, have left the League. In comparison eight of the original members of Division III (North) have left.

In Merthyr Town's last season, 1930, they conceded 135 goals. Coventry City still have a memento of their match with Merthyr that season, a cheque for their share of the receipts from a mid-week fixture at Merthyr's Penydarren Park amounting to eighteen shillings and fourpence.

Manchester United recorded their highest total in a single match on 26 September 1956 when they beat Anderlecht 10–0 in a preliminary round of the European Cup.

During the 1950s, when Peterborough United was a Midland League side, they were managed by two FA Cup winning goalkeepers: Jack Fairbrother who won with Newcastle in 1951 and George Swindon who won the cup with Arsenal in 1952.

Edgar Kail of Dulwich Hamlet was the last man to appear for England while attached to an amateur club when he played against Spain in England's 3–4 defeat in 1929.

In 1929 Alex Cheyne of Aberdeen scored the first goal direct from a corner in an international when Scotland met England at Hampden Park.

When Wigan played their 100th League match on 27 September 1981 against Mansfield Town Tommy Gore and Jeff Wright also celebrated centenaries, having played in all 100 games.

Steve Perryman was capped seventeen times for England's Under-23 side but received only one full cap when he played as substitute in the match against Northern Ireland in 1982.

In 1977 Joe Craig came on as a substitute for Scotland in their match against Sweden at Hampden Park and scored with his first touch of the ball — a header.

When David Felcate joined Lincoln City in September 1980 from Bolton Wanderers he had played his previous sixty-one games for Rochdale and Crewe, to whom he was loaned, without once playing for Bolton.

Cambridge United are the only Football League club to have achieved their record defeat and record victory against the same opposition with the same scoreline. On 18 September 1971 they beat Darlington 6–0 in a Division IV match and on 28 September 1974 Darlington reversed the score.

On 28 September 1946 Johnny Carey played for Northern Ireland having played for the Republic of Ireland only two days before; both appearances were made against England.

In an international between France and Northern Ireland in Paris in 1952 France played twelve men for a period in the first half. After Boniface had been injured a substitute took his place and France saw the half out with twelve men. They won 3–1.

Crewe's goalkeeper D. Murray conceded eleven goals on his League debut against Lincoln on 29 September 1951.

When Wolves played Portsmouth for the 1939 FA Cup final the press were fascinated to see what effect the 'monkey gland' treatment, advocated by the manager Major Frank Buckley, would have on the team. Many expected some sort of extraordinary performance from the team. However, his opposing manager put his faith in his lucky white spats. They proved to be more effective than the 'monkey glands' and Portsmouth won the cup 4–1.

Between 1966 and 1978 Bill Dodgin junior assisted five different League clubs to gain promotion: Millwall, Queen's Park Rangers, Fulham, Northampton and Brentford.

Pele's club Santos scored 338 goals from ninety-four games in 1961.

When Chic Brodie made his first appearance for Northampton Town in a Division III match on 30 September 1961 it was his third consecutive appearance in a different division. After making a League debut for Aldershot in February 1961, he was transferred to Wolves where he made one Division I appearance before the end of the season. His next appearance was in the Northampton side the following season.

Dumbarton, who won the first two Scottish Division I titles in 1891 and 1892, were known as 'Sons of the Rock'.

When he took control of the Greek side AEK Athens in 1980 Christo Bonen became the first Bulgarian footballer to move to the West.

Tunisia became the first 1978 World Cup finalists to be eliminated in the 1982 competition.

Kick-off

October is the month when England tends to have its first try-out of the season, and we are able to see the strength of the international team. It doesn't matter which club you support, each of us has half an eye on the national squad of our own country. It is a topic of conversation that can involve anyone interested in the game; we all have our ideas of who should or should not be picked.

Having been a club manager, I can appreciate how difficult it must be to be the national manager. In a club, a manager has time with players — time to establish who are the best, who are reliable, who are going to let you down under pressure and who are not. You will see, too, who are good team members and who tend to be a bit selfish when they get the ball. In a word, you have time to 'play' your hand, but with the national team this is not available. The national team manager's job is one of putting together a jigsaw puzzle and hoping the pieces fit. It may not take a lot of genius to select the best twenty-two players out of the Football League, but the skill is to take the ones who will click as a team — after little enough practice — and produce an outstanding performance, often for one isolated evening in October.

October

The first European Cup tie to be played behind closed doors took place on 1 October 1980 due to previous crowd disturbances; West Ham beat Castilla.

Leicester City's Johnny Morris was suspended for two weeks at the start of the 1957/58 season after suggesting in a practice match that the referee needed glasses.

Between 1978 and 1983 all the European Cup finals finished with a 1–0 score. In 1984 the match was decided on penalties, which Liverpool won to beat Roma. And the ill-fated Liverpool-Juventus match of 1985 resulted in a 1–0 victory for Juventus, again scored from a penalty.

Pele was injured for both the 1958 and 1962 World Cup finals.

The famous red card lasted from 2 October 1976 until 17 January 1981. The first player to be shown it was Blackburn's David Wagstaff, the last were Leyton Orient's Nigel Gray and Cardiff City's Cary Stevens who had been fighting.

On 2 October 1965 Spurs provided both goalkeepers in the match between Northern Ireland and Scotland when Pat Jennings and Bill Brown faced each other.

Ron Davies and Mike England were both born in 1942, both played in the same school side and then ended up playing alongside each other for Wales.

After drawing 0–0 with the Turkish League champions Fenerbahce at Maine Road, Manchester City, the 1968 Division I champions, travelled to Turkey for the away leg and lost their only European Cup tie 1–2 on 2 October.

3

When Bryan Robson moved from West Bromwich Albion to Manchester United the fee of £1,500,000 paid for him on 3 October 1981 set a British club record.

Hull City have never entered Division I since their founding in 1904. Their most successful season was 1909/10 when they finished third in Division II.

Liverpool's Craig Johnston has a cosmopolitan background. He was born in South Africa, brought up in Australia, had a Scottish grandfather, an Irish grandmother and he is currently a British citizen.

Arthur Wharton, the first black player in the Football League, who made appearances in the 1890s, held the AAA men's 100-yard title in 1886 and 1887.

4

Tucker scored a hat-trick making his Football League debut for West Ham against Chesterfield on 4 October 1947.

Sheffield Wednesday's inside-forward Redfern Froggatt was in their promotion sides from Division II in 1949/50, 1951/52, 1955/56 and 1958/59. However, he was also in their relegation sides of 1950/51, 1954/55 and 1957/58.

The Jewish footballer Louis Buckhalter, who played four times for Ireland between 1914 and 1922, is the only British international to play under an assumed name. In the record books he is found under L.O. Bookman.

Between 1955 and 1964 Alfredo Di Stefano scored forty-nine goals in European Cup competitions.

On 5 October 1946 Newcastle United beat Newport County 13-0 to record the greatest margin in a Football League match for the second time this century. In 1934 Stockport County achieved the same scoreline against Halifax Town.

There was a proposal in 1971 to change Bury's name to Manchester North End, but this did not meet with over-whelming popularity at Gigg Lane!

The circumstances by which Bill Corman came to play for the Republic of Ireland in fourteen internationals between 1936 and 1947 revolved around his parents' holiday plans. His father was Scottish and his mother English and Corman could not have played for Eire if they had not been on holiday in Ireland when their son was born, and stayed there for three weeks after his birth.

J.D. Ross scored seven goals for Preston North End in their match with Stoke City on 6 October 1888, establishing a record for Division I that has only once been equalled, in 1935 by Ted Drake of Arsenal against Aston Villa.

Lincoln City have experienced three spells outside the Football League. They were one of the original founders of Division II in 1892, failed to gain re-election in 1908, returned the following year, failed to gain re-admission in 1911, came back in 1912 and were out again in 1920. The following year they were founder members of Division III (North).

In October 1932 Chelsea finished one Division I game with only six players, the others having left the field through exhaustion brought on by the blizzard in which they were playing. Chelsea lost that match 0-4.

In October 1932 Chelsea played in a blizzard — and finished the match with only six players on the field.

7

When Everton visited Brighton on 7 October 1980 they became the first Football League club to play in 3,000 Division I matches.

During the 1980 season Leyton Orient had two Nigerian internationals on their staff, John Chedozie and Tunji Banjo who played in the World Cup qualifying series.

Crompton of Blackburn Rovers had an illustrious international career with a record of forty-two international appearances that lasted until beaten by Billy Wright winning his forty-third international cap against Switzerland in 1952.

Bradford were the first club to hold the current FA Cup after winning it in 1912. The first cup was stolen, of course, and the second was donated by Lord Kinnaird in 1911.

8

Between 8 October 1960 and 10 May 1961 England played six internationals and won all of them with a tally of forty goals and a deficit of only eight. The England team remained unchanged for the first five games, the only alterations being made for the final game against Mexico, which they won 8–0.

At the same time as he was managing Queen's Park Rangers, Terry Venables was co-author of a football novel *They Used To Play on Grass* with Gordon Williams, the author of *Straw Dogs*. QPR, under Venables, were the first British League club to install a synthetic playing surface.

Hamilton Academical were continuous members of Scottish League Division I, although running perilously close to relegation on a number of occasions. Their 1934/35 season was their most successful when they finished fourth in the League.

The game between Barrow and Gillingham of Division IV was abandoned fifteen minutes before time on 9 October 1961 owing to bad light. It had been late in starting after Gillingham had missed their train and had had to charter a plane to fly them north. The Football League ordered the result to stand when the game was abandoned and Barrow were leading 7–0.

Lower division football in Scotland poses special problems of its own. In the 1971/72 season Montrose were drawn to play Stranraer in the same cup section. Montrose had to travel 200 miles for the game, which meant leaving at 7.00 am on the Wednesday morning and returning twenty-two hours later after receiving match takings of £150.

During the 1962 World Cup finals England did not have an official doctor in their party and Peter Swan became seriously ill after receiving poor treatment for an illness he contracted.

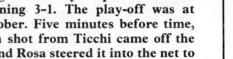

The Italian club Naples narrowly escaped one of the most sensational giant killings ever in the 1962/63 European Cup-winners' Cup competition. They were drawn against the Welsh Cup champions, the Cheshire League club Bangor City. Two of Naples' forwards, Rosa and Ticchi, had alone cost more than Bangor had earned as a club since the end of the Second World War, but in their home leg on 5 September 1962 Bangor scored an astonishing 2–0 victory. Naples levelled in the return leg, winning 3–1. The play-off was at Highbury on 10 October. Five minutes before time, with the score 1–1, a shot from Ticchi came off the Bangor goalkeeper and Rosa steered it into the net to save Naples from further humiliation.

A game of street football played every Shrove Tuesday at Ashbourne in Derbyshire has been dated back to AD 217.

Bobby Charlton's birthday.

On 11 October 1958 Spurs rewarded Bill Nicholson, their newly appointed manager, with a 10–4 defeat of Everton, equalling the previous aggregate record of fourteen goals from a Division I match which was set in 1892 when Aston Villa thrashed Accrington Stanley 12–2.

Marvin Hinton of Chelsea came on twice as a substitute in the 1970 FA Cup final.

The great Tommy Lawton was introduced to young Nat Lofthouse after his trial with Lancashire Schools and told him, 'Always try to bang in one or two Nat, and remember it's goals that count.' Lofthouse followed his advice and by his retirement in 1961 had scored 289 goals from 282 games.

Tony MacNamara played in all four divisions of the Football League within twelve months beginning with his last game for Everton on 12 October 1957. On 27 September 1958 he made his debut for Bury in Division III, having played for Liverpool in Division II and Crewe in Division IV in the meantime.

Between his signing for over £1,000,000 in 1979 and his £300,000 transfer to the American club Seattle Sounders in February 1981, Steve Daley's fifty-one League games for Manchester City cost over £22,000 each, without including bonuses.

Martin Busby and his brother Viv were both called on as substitutes in a Division II match between Queen's Park Rangers and Luton Town: Martin appearing for QPR and Viv for Luton.

Bobby Charlton was born on 11 October 1937.

On 13 October 1951 R. Parry played in Division I for Bolton Wanderers against Wolverhampton Wanderers when he was fifteen years 207 days old.

In 1922 David Calderhead became the first former professional footballer to receive a medal from the Football League for club managership.

According to one football historian, 'The only footballer to have matched the immortal W.G. Grace in being known to the public by his initials alone' was the very popular amateur centre-forward, G.O. Smith, who played for England twenty times between 1892 and 1893.

Two years before Norwich City staged their giant-killing Cup run of 1959 they were lying at the bottom of Division III (South) and were saved by a local appeal fund. One week the financial position was so desperate that the local paper had to pay their wages, according to their loyal servant Ron Ashman.

B. Joy made his final appearance for England on 14 October 1944 in their match against Scotland. As a wartime match this was not regarded as a full international. However, Joy had been the last amateur player to win a full England cap eight years earlier in a match against Belgium in Brussels.

The 1878/79 Scottish Cup competition is remembered for two controversies. Hearts failed to turn up for their match against Helensburgh and in the final the Vale of Leven were awarded the cup when Rangers refused to take part in the replay after the Scottish FA turned down their protest that they had scored a perfectly legitimate goal in their first game.

Bobby Charlton was substituted fifteen minutes from the final whistle of his last international appearance for England, the World Cup quarter-final against West Germany in 1970, which the Germans won 3–2 after extra time.

On 15 October 1887 Preston North End beat Hyde 26–0 in an FA Cup tie, the highest score between English clubs in a major competition.

Birmingham City, renowned for their defensive football, are still the only club to have scored double figures in Football League matches on five occasions: in 1892/93 (as Small Heath) beating Walsall Town 12–0, in 1893/94 beating Ardwick 10–2, in 1900/01 winning against Blackpool 10–1, in 1902/03 Doncaster Rovers were their victims with a 12–0 defeat and in 1914/15 they beat Glossop 11–1.

Ferenc Puskas became the only player to score a hat-trick in a European Cup final and finish on the losing side when Real Madrid lost 3–5 to Benfica.

Arsenal's Eddie Hapgood was the most capped English international between the two World Wars with a total of thirty appearances for his country.

Ivor Allchurch, one of the most famous names in post-Second World War football, was born on 16 October 1929. He scored 251 goals in his 694 League games.

When Blackpool signed Jimmy Hampson from Nelson in 1927 they found that their new player had gone to the cinema and had to contact him by persuading the manager to flash a message on to the screen, 'Will Jimmy Hampson please call at the manager's office immediately'. Once with the club he established records by scoring forty-five goals in a single season and creating a career total of 247 between 1927 and 1938.

In 1978 the Italian magazine *Guerin Sportivo* organized the Bravo Award for the best under twenty-four-year-old in Europe and its first winner was Jimmy Case.

Bob Paisley won an amateur FA Cup winners' medal with Bishop Auckland in 1939.

Johnny Haynes, born on 17 October 1934, became the first £100-a-week player in British football in 1961.

All five goals scored for Huddersfield Town by Jimmy Glazzard in the 8-2 victory over Everton in the 1952/53 season came from headers and all five headers came from crosses made by Vic Metcalfe.

The Yorkshire cricketer Fred Trueman played centre-forward in Lincoln City's Midland League side in 1952/53.

The former Newcastle United player Jackie Milburn, who scored 179 goals from 354 appearances between 1947 and 1957, is the uncle of Bobby and Jack Charlton.

Referee Norman Burtenshaw once sent off the entire Benfica side during a friendly match at Highbury.

Ten Division II matches were played on 18 October 1980, of which seven ended in draws and the remaining three were won by visiting teams.

Stan Mortenson scored in twelve consecutive games in the FA Cup between 1946 and 1950.

Cardiff City drew Leeds United in the third round of the FA Cup in three successive years between 1955 and 1958, winning 2-1 on each occasion.

A soft drink can made Borussia Moenchengladbach pay dearly in their 1971/72 European Cup campaign. The can was thrown at Roberto Bonionseona of Inter Milan during the first leg of their second-round match. Borussia won 7-0, but they were fined £1,000, were banned from playing European matches at home and had to replay on a neutral ground in Berlin. The Italians had won their home leg 4-2 and by drawing 0-0 in Berlin knocked Borussia out of the cup.

Jim Barrett of West Ham made his international debut for England against Northern Ireland on 19 October 1929. He played for eight minutes before being injured and carried from the field, and never played again for England.

Bobby Collins holds the record for playing in the greatest number of post-1945 British League seasons, beginning with Celtic in 1949/50 and ending with Oldham in 1972/73 — a total of twenty-three seasons.

Jimmy Jackson, who played right-back for Liverpool before the Second World War, became a congregational minister and Port Vale's Norman Hallam later became a Methodist parson.

In 1964 Alloa Athletic staged a special match at their Recreation Ground for an episode of *Dr Finlay's Casebook*.

'Let me through, I'm a television actor!'

Newcastle's W. Foulkes scored with his first kick in international football with a goal for Wales against England on 20 October 1951.

In 1971 Oldham Athletic won the only Ford Motor Company sporting League. The League's scoring system was one point for each home goal, two points for each away goal, five points deducted for each player cautioned and ten points deducted for each player sent off. Oldham scored ninety-seven points. They also finished third in the Football League Division IV.

In 1972 West German players took the first three places in the European Footballer of the Year poll: Beckenbauer was first, Muller second and Netzer third.

The Irish League club Milford lost all fourteen matches in the first season of the Irish League in 1891, scoring ten goals and conceding sixty-two. Two years later they resigned from the League.

21

Eddie Payne, a player who had been neglected by Fulham in 1892, made his debut for Spurs on 21 October 1893 and almost cost them their amateur status because of the row over his football boots. When he went to collect his kit from Fulham he found it had been stolen. Spurs kitted him out with everything he needed except boots; he was given ten shillings to buy some himself. After his first match against Old St Marks in a London FA Cup tie, Fulham accused Spurs of having poached their player and made charges of professionalism. The London FA investigated and ruled that Spurs hadn't poached Payne, but they had broken the amateurism rules. Payne had to repay the ten shillings to maintain amateur status.

Ian Rush was the youngest of six brothers who all played for Flint Town in the Clwyd League.

On 22 October 1955 Arthur Rowley was playing for Leicester against Fulham at Craven Cottage and his brother Jack was at Oakwell playing for Plymouth Argyle against Barnsley, and both completed career aggregates of 200 Football League goals.

When Terry Venables played for England against Belgium in 1964 he became the first man to represent England at all five international levels: schoolboy; youth; amateur; Under-23 and full.

In the 1967/68 season a Gold Boot Award was given to the players who scored the most goals in a season in Europe. The first winners were Eusebio with forty-three, Dumai with thirty-six and Lennox with thirty-two.

At the end of the 1973/74 season Middlesbrough were Division II champions, fifteen points clear of their nearest rivals.

Pele was born Edson Arantes do Nascimento on 23 October 1940.

On 23 October 1920 Crystal Palace's Robert McCraken became the first Division III player to play in an international when he represented Northern Ireland against England.

On 23 October 1971 Celtic experienced one of their heaviest defeats in a cup final when they lost the Scottish League Cup 1–4 to Partick Thistle.

Kerry Dixon had the disappointment of scoring four goals for Reading in their 1982 match against Doncaster and still seeing his side lose 5–7.

Pele was born Edson Arantes do Nascimento on 23 October 1940.

Hibs beat Airdrie 11–1 on 24 October 1959 to set a record away win.

East Fife's Henry Morris scored 175 goals from 190 League appearances between 1946 and 1953, yet he made only one international appearance for Scotland in their 8–2 victory over Northern Ireland in 1949. Morris scored a hat-trick that afternoon.

Only four grounds other than Wembley have staged home internationals for England in the last twenty-five years: Molyneux for the 1956 match with Denmark, Villa Park for the 1958 England-Wales match, Hillsborough in 1962 for the France-England game and Goodison Park for England's 1966 meeting with Poland.

West Bromwich Albion and Aston Villa are the only clubs to have played each other in three FA Cup finals: 1887, 1892 and 1895.

On 25 October 1958 Albert Mundy scored a goal six seconds after kick-off in a Division IV match between his club Aldershot and Hartlepool United — one of only a handful of players to achieve this feat in the history of the Football League.

Between 1958 and 1961 Wolverhampton Wanderers scored four consecutive centuries in Division I, with a total of 422 goals, 103 of which were scored by Jimmy Murray.

Stoke City retained forty-eight playing professionals in the 1942/43 season, all but four of whom were locally born.

In the very first FA competition in 1971/72 Downington School, near Spalding, Lincolnshire, were drawn to play Queen's Park Rangers in the first round. They scratched and never played in the competition again.

The former Wolves and Northampton player William Barron, who was born on 26 October 1917, also played first-class cricket for Lancashire and Northamptonshire.

In 1983 Frank Stapleton became the first player to score for two different clubs in FA Cup finals. In 1979 he scored for Arsenal against Manchester United and four years later he scored for Manchester United against Brighton.

Since 1925/26 Yeovil have appeared in the first round of the FA Cup proper on thirty-six occasions.

Swansea Town had four pairs of brothers on their books during the 1953/54 season: Cyril and George Beech; Bryn and Cliff Jones; Ivor and Ken Allchurch and Colin and Alan Hole.

Just one month after achieving Football League status in October 1903 Bradford City's ground Valley Parade hosted the inter-League match between the Football League and the Irish League.

Between September 1956 and April 1957 Crewe Alexandra went for thirty games without a win.

The very first game in the first Scottish FA Cup competition was between Kilmarnock and Renton in October 1873. Kilmarnock lost 0–3 for reasons outlined in the report in the *Glasgow Evening News*: 'Kilmarnock were at a disadvantage through not being thoroughly conversant with Association rules, having formerly played the rugby game, and being one man short.'

Bobby Evans, who for thirteen years played for Celtic, winning forty-eight Scottish caps, spent the next eight seasons with five different clubs until he retired in 1968.

Nottingham Forest were beaten 1–2 on 28 October 1878 in a match with a Birmingham representative side under artificial light, provided by a dozen electric lights spaced out around the pitch.

It was not until 1951 that Northern Ireland played their first international against foreign opposition when they played France in a 2–2 draw in Belfast. Their first away match was against France, in Paris.

Burton, famous for its brewing industry, supported two Football League clubs in the 1890s. Neither exists today.

In the 1968/69 season Les Allen became the first player-manager in Division I since the Second World War, with Queen's Park Rangers.

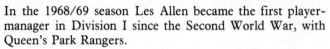

Barrow signed two Argentinian players in October 1937, Augustus Corpa at half-back and inside-left Casco Rinaldi.

Since the Second World War Walter Galbraith has been manager of three clubs that are no longer in the Football League: New Brighton, Accrington Stanley and Bradford Park Avenue.

Aberdeen's ground, Pittodrie (which in Gaelic means 'hill of dung'), opened as the UK's first all-seated ground in 1978.

After leaving school Eddie Hapgood was driving a horse-drawn milk float in his native Bristol where he was spotted playing football by Bristol Rovers who offered him £8 a week during the season, but wanted him to drive a coal cart in the summer. He turned it down in favour of non-League Kettering's offer of £14 a week in season and £3 out of it, until Herbert Chapman signed him for Arsenal.

The first Welsh Cup tie was held on 30 October 1877 when the Druids of Ruabon played Newton.

Carlisle United have had the youngest and oldest first-time managers in the Football League since 1945. In 1946 Ivor Broadis joined them as manager aged twenty-three and thirty years later Dick Young became the oldest first-time manager in the history of the League.

During a Division I match in 1976 against Leicester in 1976, Aston Villa's Chris Nicholl scored two goals for each side — emulating a feat achieved by Sam Wynne of Oldham playing against Manchester United in 1923.

In 1900 Kettering was the first non-League club to apply to the Football League for membership; they received two votes. In 1927 they applied again and got one vote.

During the match between the Scottish League and the Irish League at Firhill Park, Glasgow, on 31 October 1928 B. Battles scored five goals for the Scottish League.

Joe Baker and Chris Crowe shared the distinction of having played for both Scottish Schools and England.

Two division III Players, W. Rawlings and F. Titmuss, both from Southampton, played for England in their 1922 match with Wales.

The first English club to win the European Cup was Manchester United with their victory over Benfica in 1968 when Alex Stepney saved a shot from Eusebio at point blank range just before the end of the game, with the score at 1–1. In extra time three Manchester goals gave them a 4–1 victory. Brian Kidd scored in that game on his nineteenth birthday.

Kick-off

November is renowned as the month when fog affects football, and the episode that brought this home to me was a match we played at Coventry one November evening against Barnsley. We were 2–0 up when the fog came down, and threatened our chances of an important win. We were in a good position in the League and thought we had a chance of promotion, so the points from this game were vital. The referee came into the dressing-room with different coloured flags to see if they were going to be visible from the pitch. But the fog was getting thicker and thicker and after twenty-five minutes the teams were brought off, although the referee said that if it cleared he would be prepared to resume play.

This left us with a crowd in the stands and nothing to entertain them. It was just after we had written the 'Sky Blues Song', the Coventry City club song which we were busy promoting on the lines of:

> *Let's all sing together,*
> *Play up, Sky Blues,*
> *While we sing together,*
> *We will never lose,*

sung to the tune of the 'Eton Boating Song'.

It so happened that Derek Robins, the Coventry chairman at that time, had performed in amateur opera on the local stage. So we decided to introduce the song to the stands, and for the only time in history, I should imagine, the chairman of a football club sang over the public address system while the club manager (me) stood in front of the stands and conducted the spectators as they joined in with the words he shouted out to them.

In the end the game had to be abandoned, but we had the satisfaction of teaching the song to a good proportion of the supporters — and we won the replay.

November

Jimmy Scarth scored a hat-trick for Gillingham in two and a half minutes in their Division III (South) match with Leyton Orient on 1 November 1952.

Major Frank Buckley of 'monkey gland' fame was still a manager in the Football League with Walsall in his seventy-third year. He played for England in one international in 1914 while he was with Derby County, at centre-half against Northern Ireland.

Between 1908 and 1935 Norwich City, nicknamed 'Canaries', played at the 'Nest', Rosary Road before moving to Carrow Road.

In the 1979/80 season Clive Allen became the youngest Football League leading scorer with twenty-eight goals for Queen's Park Rangers. He had just passed his nineteenth birthday.

Colin Stein scored a hat-trick in three minutes for Rangers in their match with Arbroath in the Scottish League Division I on 2 November 1968.

West Bromwich Albion is the only current Division I club not to have been knocked out by a non-League club in the FA Cup.

As part of his strategy for winning the 1966 World Cup Alf Ramsey insisted on taking full control of selection and made the selectors virtually redundant. When one of them asked him at a cocktail party what they were meant to do, he told him: 'Attend cocktail parties.'

The word 'gornik' which is part of the name of one of Poland's leading football clubs, Gornik Zabrze, means 'miner' in Polish.

3

On 3 November 1969 the referee of a game between Tongham Youth Club and Hawley booked all twenty-two players and one of the linesmen.

Gerd Muller, whose birthday is 3 November, scored thirty-six European Cup goals for Bayern Munich between 1969 and 1970.

The most prolific scorer in British football in the Second World War was Newcastle United's Albert Stubbins who between 1939 and 1945 scored 245 goals from 199 games. Having been brought up in the USA he returned there in 1960 to become their national coach.

It took eighteen seasons for a second Division I player to score five goals in a single match away from home. The first had been Bobby Tambling playing for Chelsea against Aston Villa in 1966. In the 1983/84 season Tony Woodcock repeated this feat, also at Villa Park.

4

John Jones, his brother Samuel Jones and their brother-in-law William Mitchell played as England's half-back line in the international against Wales on 4 November 1933.

Only three clubs, Notts Forest, Leicester City and Birmingham City, have scored over thirty goals in both Division I and Division II.

In 1886 Charles Heggie was credited with five goals for Scotland against England in his only international appearance.

In the 1937/38 season Raith Rovers scored 142 goals in Scottish League Division II, the highest number by any British League club.

After weeks of negotiation by the Arsenal manager Herbert Chapman Gillespie Road underground station on London's Piccadilly Line had its name changed to Arsenal on 5 November 1932.

In 1965 Wolves threatened the BBC with a court injunction claiming that the new drama series *United* was a thinly-disguised version of their recent troubles.

In 1968 Bristol Rovers' fan Gordon Bennett was awarded the title of Britain's Number One Football Fan and won £1,000 and a trip to Mexico to watch the World Cup. He proved himself worthy of the title by donating his £1,000 prize to the club, in the hope that it might enable them to set up a youth team.

Bela Guttman, who piloted Benfica to their European Cup successes of the 1960s, was a dancing master by profession.

On 6 November 1948 Joe Cockcroft made his Division I debut for Sheffield United against Preston North End at the age of thirty-eight years five months.

At the outbreak of the Second World War Derby County had players in the ranks who were leading goal-scorers for England (Steve Bloomer), Wales (D. Astley) and Scotland (H. Gallacher).

The 1945/46 FA Cup was run on a two-legged system. Going into their home leg Barnsley were 2–4 down to Newcastle United. In anticipation of a record crowd at the mid-week match the local collieries put up a notice reading, 'In order that the management may have knowledge of numbers to be absent on Wednesday afternoon, will those whose relatives are to be buried on the day please apply by Tuesday for permission to attend.' There were 27,000 funerals and Barnsley honoured their dead with a 3–0 victory.

'Now remember, lads, when you get in their penalty area, point those toes!'

7 November 1907 was Edward VII's birthday, celebrated with special enthusiasm by workers at the Royal Arsenal works at Woolwich, which closed for the day, also the date of the first all-London clash in the Division I, when Woolwich Arsenal met Chelsea at Stamford Bridge. Arsenal won 2–1, thanks to the huge Arsenal following that accounted for a large portion of the 65,000 present to watch the game.

Tom Phillipson, who played centre-forward for Wolves when they became Division III (North) champions in 1924, was later to become Lord Mayor of Wolverhampton.

Hugo Meisl, the mastermind behind the famous Austrian Wunderteam that beat Scotland 5–0 and West Germany 6–0 in the early 1930s, also instigated a competition for the top central European nations, of which Italy became the first winners.

Stenhousemuir staged the first floodlit football match in Scotland in November 1951.

Dick Pym played in goal for Bolton Wanderers in the 1923, 1926 and 1929 FA Cup final winning sides and never conceded a goal.

Brian Clough went to Hartlepool for his first managerial appointment and in 1968, his second season, took them out of Division IV for the first time in their history.

Peterborough were relegated in 1968 for illegal payments but Mansfield, who had finished twenty-first in Division III, stayed up. Peterborough had been ninth in the division that year.

⑨

Jack Balmer of Liverpool is the only player in the history of the Football League to have scored hat-tricks (or more) on three successive Saturdays. He began his record-making run on 9 November 1946 with a hat-trick against Portsmouth, the following week scored four goals against Derby County and on 23 November he got another hat-trick, against Arsenal.

Blackpool's Stan Mortenson made his international debut in a match at Wembley during the Second World War when he appeared for Wales! Although he was England's reserve, he went on as the second-half substitute for the injured Welsh half-back Ivor Powell.

The Bulgarian international Asparovkov, who played for his country forty-nine times in the 1960s, turned down the chance to join Benfica.

⑩

On 10 November 1888 Preston North End dropped a point at home to Aston Villa, one of only four points they dropped in that whole season that saw them play twenty-two Division matches without a defeat.

In 1888 however, Preston were beaten in the FA Cup final by West Brom, who were the first club to field a cup-winning team comprised entirely of Englishmen.

In the mid-1950s Manchester City used Don Revie as a deep-lying centre-forward, just as the Hungarians used Hideguti. Both were an instant success.

P. Cea scored the equalizer for Uruguay in the 1930 World Cup final, having also scored equalizers in the 1924 and 1928 Olympic finals.

Ron Greenwood, whose birthday is 11 November, used to be a signwriter and once spent part of the close season painting names on the doors of dressing-rooms, offices and the board room at Brentford's Griffin Park.

The last FA Cup final before they were staged at Wembley from 1923 was also the first to be decided by a penalty when Billy Smith scored for Huddersfield against Preston.

John O'Hare was Brian Clough's first signing at Derby when he joined in the 1967/68 season for £23,000 from Sunderland.

In addition to having Rattin sent off in the World Cup quarter-final against England, Argentina also had Albrecht sent off in their match with West Germany.

The first half-back to score a hat-trick in the Football League was Robertson of Small Heath who got three goals against Luton Town in their Division II match on 12 November 1898.

Exeter City have never risen beyond Division III although they were runners-up to Brentford in Division III (South) in the 1932/33 season.

Arsenal won the 1950 FA Cup without having to travel outside London to play a match.

In the 1889 England-Scotland match Blackburn's James Forest became the first professional footballer to play for England.

On 13 November 1915 Celtic began a run of sixty-two matches which they either won or drew that lasted until 21 April 1917. During this unbeaten period they won 49 games and drew thirteen.

The fastest goal ever scored in an FA Cup final was the one that ricocheted off John Dewey of Aston Villa and went into the West Brom goal thirty seconds after the start of the 1895 final.

At the end of the 1927/28 season only sixteen points separated Everton, the League champions, from Middlesbrough at the bottom of Division I; in fact the bottom nine clubs were separated by just two points.

El Salvador reached the 1970 World Cup finals after ten matches and a three-day war with Honduras.

Bobby Moore made his 108th and final England appearance against Italy at Wembley on 14 November 1973.

Thirty-nine years earlier to the day England had played Italy as well, though the match was held at Highbury. For seven of the England team, all Arsenal players, this was very much a home match.

Nottingham Forest were knocked out of their first season in Europe on a slight technicality in the European Fairs Cup on 14 November 1967. After winning the home leg 2–1 they travelled to Switzerland to play the away leg against FC Zurich, which Notts lost 0–1. However, while the Swiss team left the field in jubilation at the end of the game, ten red shirts stood in the middle of the pitch waiting for the extra time that never came. As Terry Hennessy later confessed, 'We didn't know the rules.'

On 15 November 1950 Leslie Compton became the oldest player to make his England debut when he was picked to play against Wales at the age of thirty-eight.

Between 1946 and 1955 Southampton had three different managers: Bill Dodgin senior, Sid Cann and George Roughton. But in the last thirty years they have had just two managers: Ted Bates and Laurie McMenemy.

In 1894 Notts County became the first Division II club to win the FA Cup. Since then six other clubs from Division II have followed them: Wolves in 1908; Barnsley in 1912; West Brom in 1931; Sunderland in 1973; Southampton in 1976; and West Ham in 1980.

Between 1910 and 1912 Bradford City went for twelve consecutive FA Cup ties without conceding a goal.

In the first-round FA Cup tie on 16 November 1878 between Notts Forest and Notts County, Forest included three Cursham brothers and three Greenhalgh brothers.

Willie Hall of Spurs scored five goals for England against Ireland on 16 November 1938 including the fastest international hat-trick, achieved in three and a half minutes.

In 1930 Manchester United lost their first twelve League Division I games.

When Ipswich town won the FA Cup in 1978 it was their second appearance at Wembley. They had won their first game in October 1928 playing Ealing Association in a Southern League fixture at Wembley because Ealing's own ground was unfit for use. On that occasion Ipswich won 4–0 in front of a crowd of 1,200.

Nottingham Forest's run of fifty-one Division I home wins came to an end on 17 November 1979 when they lost 0–1 to Brighton, who were then lying bottom of the division.

The oldest Football League programme still in existence is believed to be that for the first match of the 1893/94 season played by Preston North End against Derby County.

Liverpool have played more games in Europe than any other British club.

Andrade, who won a World Cup winners' medal for Uruguay in 1950, had an uncle who won one for Uruguay twenty years earlier.

The England-Hungary match of 18 November 1981 set a record for earnings from a British international football match with £671,000.

R. Orsi, who played outside-left in the 1930 World Cup final for Argentina, went one better four years later and played outside-left for the champions, Italy.

When Jim Baxter joined Notts Forest from Sunderland in November 1967 he was the first £100,000 defender in English football.

In 1909 Billy Meredith won an FA Cup winners' medal with Manchester United, having won one with Manchester City five years earlier.

(19)

Pele scored his 1000th goal (a penalty) on 19 November 1969 when playing for Santos in his 909th first-class match.

The white ball came into official use in 1951.

There were a record 242 sending-offs in British domestic football in the 1982/83 season.

In 1922 Falkirk was one of the first Scottish clubs to buy a Football League player when they acquired Syd Puddefoot from West Ham.

(20)

On 20 November 1971 Ted McDougall set up an FA Cup goal-scoring record when he kicked nine goals in Bournemouth's 11–0 win over Margate.

Nottingham Forest are holders of two goal-scoring records: their 14–0 victory over Charlton in the first round of the FA Cup in 1890/91 was the biggest away win in English first-class football; and their 12–0 win over Leicester Fosse in 1909 stands as the greatest Division I victory.

The potential of the Brazilian football team first came to prominence after Chelsea's 1930 tour of Latin America which brought back admiring reports of the state of the game in South America.

Between 1948 and 1952 Manchester United's Jack Rowley played for England on four occasions in six different positions!

(21)

The first match ever postponed at Wembley was the England-Bulgaria game of 21 November 1979, which was cancelled until the following day because of fog.

During the big freeze of 1963 Halifax Town turned their pitch into an ice rink and charged the public half-a-crown a head to skate there, while the club secretary, Norman Howe, played pop music over the public address system and sold tea at sixpence a cup.

Non-League Hereford have reached the first round of the FA Cup on twenty-one occasions.

Billy Meredith was the oldest player to take part in an FA Cup match when he took to the field with Manchester City against Newcastle in a semi-final just four months short of his fiftieth birthday.

(22)

After England's run of seventeen international victories Yugoslavia became the first side to escape defeat when they forced a 2–2 draw at Highbury on 22 November 1950.

Of the forty-three English and Scottish clubs that have played in Europe only Morton, beaten twice by Chelsea in 1968/69, have failed to win in Europe.

During the 1978/79 winter the Scottish Cup tie between Inverness Thistle and Falkirk had to be postponed twenty-nine times.

The 1915 FA Cup final between Sheffield United and Chelsea was nicknamed the Khaki Final because of the thousands of servicemen who packed in to see it.

On 23 November 1966 Shamrock Rovers were just eighteen minutes away from knocking Bayern Munich out of the European Cup-winners' Cup. Following a 1–1 draw at home, they were deadlocked at 2–2 in Munich with the minutes ticking away. Then Gerd Muller scored the winner that gave Bayern Munich a place in the final in which they won their first major European trophy.

Stan Seymour scored the winning goal for Newcastle United in the 1924 FA Cup final and twenty-eight years later managed them to win the 1952 FA Cup final.

In the 1952/53 season the entire Huddersfield defence played in all of their forty-two League matches.

A.G. Bowser of the Corinthians was the last amateur to captain a full England international team when they faced Wales in 1927.

In November 1978 Viv Anderson became the first black footballer to play for England in a full international when he was picked to play against Czechoslovakia.

In 1975 Chester became the last of the original surviving members of Division IV to be promoted to Division III, when coming fourth.

According to one legend a gipsy curse was placed on Derby's Baseball Ground after a band of travelling people were moved from the site when construction work began. The impact this had on the club's performance is uncertain, but before the 1946 FA Cup final the Derby captain visited a gipsy encampment to make amends and his side won their match 4–1.

Danilo, who played for Brazil in the 1950 World Cup finals, had broken both his legs in a car accident nine years earlier.

When Hungary beat England 6–3 on 25 November 1953, Buzansky was the only member of the Hungarian team attached to a provincial club.

Alf Ramsey played his last international for England in that Hungary match, being replaced by R.T. Staniforth of Huddersfield in the next England international.

The England team that met Hungary on 25 November 1953 also included four Blackpool players, three of them in the forward line and one at centre-half.

The Charles brothers, Mel and John, and the Allchurch brothers, Ivor and Len, played together in three internationals for Wales in 1955 against Brazil, Northern Ireland and Israel.

The day after England's 6–3 defeat by Hungary Geoffrey Green wrote in *The Times,* 'English football can be proud of its past, but it must awake to a new future.' Until that match the Hungarians were virtually unknown in England, although they were the Olympic champions.

The numbering of players became compulsory in 1939.

The 1947 FA Cup tie between Charlton Athletic and Bristol Rovers was the first FA Cup match, other than a final, to be televized.

When Tommy Docherty addressed the Aston Villa board for the first time he told them, 'I'd love to stay at Villa Park for the rest of my career, but in football who can tell?' Who indeed? He stayed 397 days.

When Cameron Evans joined Sheffield United from Glasgow Rangers in November 1968 he stayed two days and played in one Central League match before returning north to join Kilmarnock because he was homesick.

Jimmy McGrory scored 397 goals in fourteen seasons for Celtic and then managed Kilmarnock in his first season with them in 1938 to beat Celtic and reach the Scottish Cup final. Then he returned to Celtic after the Second World War and became their manager before Jock Stein.

Sir Stanley Rous was President of FIFA from 1961 to 1974 before being replaced by Joao Havelange.

In 1931 Notts County's Tom Keetley scored hat-tricks in three successive Division II away matches.

On 28th November 1955 Carlisle United and Darlington played the first FA Cup replay under floodlights at Newcastle.

A group of local spiritualists predicted in 1971 that York City would reach an FA Cup final by 1980. Sadly their prediction fell some way short of the mark, although York did manage to achieve promotion to Division II for the first time in 1974.

Founded in 1881, the Scottish club Albion Rovers come from the town of Coatbridge.

Liverpool have won six European tournaments: four European Cups in 1977, 1978, 1981 and 1984; and two UEFA Cups in 1973 and 1976. Phil Neal and Ray Clemence each played in five of these victorious sides.

The match between West Bromwich Albion and Everton on 29 November 1913 was the centre of a case of attempted bribery, when J. Remington, the West Brom captain, was offered £55 (£5 for each of the team), if they lost or drew the game. Remington got the offer stated in writing and gave it to the police who were on hand to arrest the briber at the pay-off after the game ended in a draw. He was given five months in prison.

A match played between Preston North End and Hyde in 1887 not only resulted in a record 26–0 win for Preston, but the referee also reputedly lost his watch during the game and it lasted two hours.

When England played Wales at Cardiff in 1959, Ron Flowers was the oldest member of the side at the age of twenty-five.

The first England-Scotland international was played in Glasgow on 30 November 1872 and ended in a 0–0 draw.

Wigan Athletic were elected to the Football League in 1978 but as a non-League side they had beaten Carlisle 6–1 in a 1934/35 FA Cup tie.

Rochdale did not progress beyond the first round of the FA Cup between 1928 and 1946.

The Division II match between Charlton Athletic and Walsall at the end of the 1962/63 season was going to decide which of the two would be relegated. Walsall needed a draw and Charlton a win. In the event Charlton won 2–1 and Walsall were relegated by 0.053 of a point. For Charlton's manager, Frank Hill, it was some compensation for his defeat with Arsenal in the 1933 FA Cup final which Walsall had won.

Kick-off

December means shopping time, and small Saturday afternoon gates for football clubs. It also means Christmas, and the two matches that are crammed in over the holiday; in the past these were on Christmas Day and Boxing Day. If they fell near a Saturday we were back to the same position as at Easter, with three games in four days; sometimes three games in three days! The public always turned out in large numbers then, and several clubs have recorded their highest attendances at a Christmas game.

One year, Fulham had to travel down to Plymouth over Christmas; and we played a couple of matches on consecutive days. We emerged with three points, which was not bad going after our long train ride. The team then had our own little Christmas in a holiday resort, two days after everyone else in Christendom, and I was persuaded to do an imitation of Tommy Cooper for the hotel show. He was just starting to make a name for himself, and I found I could laugh like him! I remember trying the trick of making a canary disappear from under a tea cup, and I got so confused with what I was doing that I completely lost track of which cup it really was under.

So for married players with families, Christmas could be rather a disappointing time. There was also the irony that, as a lad, I had sometimes been given a new football or a pair of boots for Christmas, but I was never allowed to try these out on Christmas Day itself because it wasn't thought right to play football on the Lord's birthday, then — when I grew up — I had found I had to play football then whether I liked it or not!

December

Stanley Matthews scored only one hat-trick in his illustrious career and that came in England's match against Czechoslovakia on 1 December 1937, which England won 5–4.

West Bromwich Albion's forward J. Haynes played in one international for England against Switzerland on 1 December 1948 and scored twice.

Gillingham's S. Raleigh died from concussion sustained in a match with Brighton on 1 December 1934.

Only one FA Cup tie has been played in Scotland, the semi-final replay between Queen's Park and Notts Forest in the 1884/85 season, which was played in Edinburgh with Queen's Park winning 3–0.

The Professional Footballer's Association was formed on 2 December 1907.

Jim Standen, who played in goal for West Ham in the 1964 FA Cup final, also won a County Championship winners' medal playing cricket for Worcestershire.

In the early days of organized football the throw-in rule caused considerable problems. In one match before 1882 England refused to take to the field against Scotland unless the referee allowed them to throw the ball as they liked. He agreed and found that the English version was a single-arm hurl that could carry the ball the full length of the pitch. This was perfected with devastating effect by the England cricketer William Gunn who played football for Notts County.

3

The nearest thing to an all-Manchester Wembley final came in the 1969/70 League Cup competition when all ninety-two clubs entered for the first time and Manchester City found themselves drawn against Manchester United on 3 December 1969. City edged home the winner after two closely-fought legs at Maine Road and Old Trafford.

In the 1951/52 season Derek Dooley scored forty-six Division II goals for Sheffield Wednesday in only thirty games. In the following two seasons he played fifty-nine games from which he scored sixty-two goals until he broke his leg in February 1953 in a match against Preston and never played again.

Only one player has been unlucky enough to miss a penalty in an FA Cup final; that was Charlie Wallace of Aston Villa when they played Sunderland in the final in 1913.

4

On 4 December 1982 Bristol City were lying at the bottom of Division IV. Three years and ninety-five days earlier they were lying sixth in Division I. In the intervening period they had dropped eighty-six places in the Football League.

Preston's J. Mitchell is the only player to have taken part in an FA Cup final wearing glasses when he kept goal against Huddersfield in 1922.

Between the 1956/57 and 1961/62 seasons Ipswich Town rose from Division III (South) to become Division I champions.

England's George Gamsell ended his international career with the best average figures ever attained by a British international. He played for England on nine occasions between 1929 and 1936 and scored a total of eighteen goals!

On **Saturday 5 December** 1908 Newcastle United, leaders of Division I, were holding their local rivals Sunderland to a 1-1 draw at St James's Park with only twenty-eight minutes of the match remaining. However, when the final whistle blew Sunderland left the field the winners with a 9-1 victory, having scored eight goals in those twenty-eight minutes.

Tommy Docherty resigned as manager of Queen's Park Rangers on 5 December 1968 having spent twenty-nine days at the club.

Before the 1984/85 season the north-east local derby was all square with thirty-eight wins each for Newcastle and Sunderland and thirty draws.

On their way to the 1974/75 FA Cup final Fulham played eleven matches and eighteen and a half hours' football, the greatest number by any FA Cup finalists.

On **6 December** 1882 Major Mandarin chaired a meeting between representatives of the English, Scottish, Welsh and Irish football associations to standardize the laws of the game once and for all.

Doncaster Rovers boast the largest playing area in the Football League, 119 by 79 yards.

Blackpool had a remarkable record in the 1948 FA Cup final. They reached Wembley without a replay and having conceded just one goal and then lost the cup 2-4 to Manchester United.

Between 1953 and 1962 Leeds United were knocked out of the FA Cup at the first hurdle in ten consecutive seasons.

On 7 December Ken Barnes, the father of Peter Barnes, scored a hat-trick of penalties for Manchester City against Everton.

Only two teams have entered the FA Cup every year since its inception: Maidenhead and Marlow.

When Hungary beat England 7–1 in Budapest in 1954, Ted Bergin, the England reserve goalkeeper commented ruefully, 'They were like men from another planet.'

Jimmy Armfield, who played full-back for Blackpool from 1955 to 1971, with 568 appearances and forty-three international caps, said of Stanley Matthews: 'I believe every kid should try to see Stanley before he retires to learn how to be a gentleman on the field.'

'I say, old chap, after you!'

Norman Hunter became the first man to win his first England cap as a substitute when he went on to replace Joe Baker in a match against Spain on 8 December 1965.

Alf Ramsey's winning 4–3–3 formula was launched in Madrid on the night of 8 December 1965 when England beat Spain 2–0. Apart from Geoff Hurst and Martin Peters, the side that won that match was the same that won the World Cup the following summer.

Geoff Hurst, whose birthday is on 8 December, was the last player to score six goals in a Football League match (against Sunderland) in Division I.

In 1965 Albert Johansson became the first black player to appear in an FA Cup final when he played for Leeds against Liverpool.

On 9 December 1978 Nottingham Forest came to the end of a run of forty-two consecutive Division I matches in which they had been unbeaten since 20 November 1977.

The 1945/46 season saw the introduction of two-legged FA Cup ties for the only time in the history of the competition, with the exception of the final, which Charlton Athletic reached that year in spite of having lost to Fulham en route.

Peter McWilliam, the Spurs manager in 1921, became the first man to play for and manage FA Cup-winning teams, having played for Newcastle in the cup-winning side of 1900.

Nick Lazarus, the son of the former Queen's Park Rangers player Mark Lazarus, once challenged Steve Davis in the one-frame Cockney Classic Snooker Tournament, and won it, collecting £1,000 in prize money.

Port Vale had a number of reasons to explain their 10–0 defeat by Sheffield United on 10 December 1892. The pitch was covered in snow; the game was played in a howling snow storm; and the Port Vale goalkeeper lost his glasses.

Celtic have always refused to number their players' shirts, although they do number their shorts.

Scotland last fielded an all-Scottish League national team in their 1966 match with the Netherlands which they lost 0–3. No Celtic player was picked for that losing side although the club was to win the Scottish League, the Scottish FA Cup and the Scottish League Cup, not to mention the European Cup only twelve months later.

Turkey's 1–0 win over Albania in 1982 marked their first win in three years and only the second goal they had scored in that time.

—— (11) ——

On 11 December 1909 Vivian Woodward equalled the record individual score in an amateur international when he scored six goals for England against the Netherlands.

In 1924 Newcastle's right-back William Hampson became the oldest player to appear in an FA Cup final at Wembley at the age of forty-one years and eight months.

J. Price of the Druids was the first Welshman to score four goals in an international when Wales played Ireland in 1882.

In 1958 Ernie Taylor appeared in his third Wembley FA Cup final in eight years having already gained winners' medals with Newcastle United in 1951, and with Blackpool in 1953. In 1958 he had to settle for a runners-up medal with Manchester United.

On 12 December 1953 a record crowd of 27,500 went to Wigan's ground at Springfield Park to watch their FA Cup second-round match against Hereford United.

Joe Smith, who scored for Bolton Wanderers in the first Wembley Cup final in 1923, returned thirty years later as the manager of Blackpool to see them beat his old club 4–3 and win the cup.

Crewe Alexandra have the distinction of being founder members of three different divisions: Division II, Division III (North) and Division IV, although between 1896 and 1922 they played non-League football.

When Middlesbrough played the Lancaster Regiment in an amateur Cup semi-final in 1895 only one spectator accompanied them to the Midlands and the team cheered him as he got off the train. Middlesbrough won 4–0.

Playing in a French league game S. Stanis scored sixteen goals in the match held on 13 December 1942.

On 13 December 1950 Scotland were beaten 0–1 by Austria, their first defeat at Hampden Park by a foreign team. Eighteen years earlier Austria had been the first nation to defeat Scotland, with a 5–0 win in Vienna.

Nottingham Forest's FA Cup victory in 1959 proved a personal triumph for their manager Billy Walker who was the League's longest-serving manager, and who had previously managed Sheffield Wednesday to win the cup in 1935.

The 1955/56 season saw the only four-way tie in the home international championship with each country finishing with three points.

When **Ted Drake scored seven goals for Arsenal against Aston Villa on 14 December 1935 he became only the second player to reach this total in Division I. The first had been James Ross of Preston North End in their match with Stoke City in October 1888.**

Between 1952 and 1962 Danny Blanchflower played in thirty-three consecutive home internationals for Northern Ireland.

The Wanderers dominated the FA Cup in its early years, winning the competition five times in the first seven seasons.

For many years Watford were sponsored by Benskins the brewers, who helped to buy their ground at Vicarage Road and kindly overlooked the loan for thirty-five years. They also matched every pound collected by the supporters' club.

England beat Luxembourg 9–0 on 15 December 1982, the highest score in any European Championship match.

In addition to England's record score on 15 December 1982, Wales were involved in an equally memorable match on the same day when they held Yugoslavia to a 4–4 draw, the highest scoring draw in a European Championship match.

In 1940 Stanley Matthews played in a cup match for Morton against Dundee United.

When Stanley Matthews moved back to Stoke after playing for Blackpool for fifteen years the transfer fee of £2,800 was made up by the gate money on his first appearance when 35,975 fans saw them beat Huddersfield 3–0. This represented a rise in numbers of 27,565 over their previous home game against Preston.

In December 1951 Freddie Steele became the first player-manager to be transferred when he moved from Mansfield to Port Vale.

In the 1966/67 season Clyde finished third behind Rangers and Celtic in the Scottish League Division I, but were denied entry to the European Fairs Cup competition on the one city one club rule.

Willie Andrews, who played three times for Northern Ireland (once in 1908 and twice in 1913), had no British qualifications. Neither he nor his parents were born in the UK. He was born in Kansas City, Missouri.

Albion Rovers' chairman Tom Fagan made good use of Third Lanark's resignation from the Scottish League in 1967. He bought 2,900 seats in their defunct ground at Cathkin Park, sold 1,900 of them at a profit, installed 600 in the stand at Cliftonville and used the other 400 in the balcony of the clubhouse.

17

Ray Wilson, who celebrates his birthday on this date, retired from professional football in 1971 and went into business as an undertaker.

Writing in 1915, Sir Walter Scott, a keen football fan himself, had this to say about the game:

> Then strip lads, and to it, though sharp be the weather,
> And if, by mischance you should happen to fall,
> There are worse things in life than a tumble on the heather,
> And life is itself a game of football.

The 1953 Cup final was one of the most nostalgic ever played and marked the occasion when Stanley Matthews was presented with his gold medal. The match also featured the first FA Cup final hat-trick scored by another Stanley, Stanley Mortenson.

This day is the birthday of the former Arsenal and Coventry City player Don Bennet, who during his career also played first class-cricket for Middlesex.

Five penalties were awarded in the 1930 World Cup game between Argentina and Mexico.

Two points separated the top four teams in Division I at the end of the 1947/47 season with one match to play for each team to decide the championship. Liverpool ended top having won an extra point, Manchester United came second, Wolves were third and Stoke City, who had been level on points with Liverpool before their final game, came fourth.

The Hearts player Andy Black scored the club's first hat-trick in a match with Rangers at Ibrox Park in the 1937/38 season.

In 1884 Blackburn became the first Football League club to win the FA Cup with a 2–1 victory. Two years later they made their FA Cup wins a hat-trick, with Brown having scored in all three finals.

Southampton and Leeds United played a League Cup match in December 1960 which did not finish until 10 pm thanks to a sixty-two minute power failure.

Until 1985 no player had been sent off during an FA Cup final, but three players have been sent off in semi-finals: Mick Martin in 1978 became the first since A. Childs had been sent off in 1930, and in 1980 Brian Kidd made the tally three.

Two British internationals were sent off in the World Cup qualifying matches in Poland. Alan Ball· was sent off at Chorzow in June and three months later Trevor Hockey of Wales left the field at Katowice.

In the match between Partick Thistle and Queen of the South on 20 December 1947 Sharp of Partick Thistle scored after just seven seconds of play.

1978 saw the only appearance of the Debenham Trophy which was awarded for the team outside Divisions I and II that progressed the furthest in the FA Cup competition. The non-League side Blyth Spartans emerged the winners after beating Wrexham 3–2 on aggregate.

Derby County's Barry Powell was picked to play for Wales's Under-23 side in 1974 only to find he was ineligible because he had played just ten minutes for the England Youth side two years earlier.

Between 1953 and 1965 Stirling Albion won the Scottish Division II title on four occasions.

On 21 December 1957 Huddersfield were leading Charlton Athletic 5–1 in their Division II match and with half an hour to go their victory seemed almost certain. The game suddenly burst into life in those closing minutes, though, and in spite of scoring a further goal, Huddersfield found themselves beaten 7–6 by a rejuvenated Charlton side. Five of Charlton's goals came from Johnny Summers.

Airdrieonians were undefeated at home in the Scottish League between September 1922 and December 1925. Between the 1922/23 and 1925/26 seasons they were runners-up in the Scottish League Division I every year.

Dixie Dean, who was never one for team talks, walked in after one defeat, put his feet up on a table, commented: 'It's this lot, they can't bloody play' and dozed off.

'Oy, Dixie, team talk's over!'

Charles Rutter, who was born on 22 December 1927, was the first player to appear for an English representative side when not attached to an English club. In 1952 he was picked for England 'B' to play the Netherlands 'B' side.

When Danny Blanchflower was introducing the Duchess of Kent to the 1961 Spurs team before the FA Cup final against Leicester City the Duchess commented: 'The other team have their names on their tracksuits.' 'But we know each other,' replied the Spurs captain.

The 'Battle of Santiago' in the 1962 World Cup finals was notorious for the punch by the Chilean player Leonel Sanchez that broke the nose of Humberto Maschio of Italy. The television audience and the crowd in the stadium saw the incident clearly, but it was missed by both linesmen and the referee. Chile won the match 2–0.

Three wise officials.

The comedian Charlie Wiliams, who played for Doncaster Rovers between 1954 and 1958, was born on 23 December 1928.

When Tommy Harmer scored the goal that lifted Chelsea back into Division I in 1963 in their 1–0 promotion tussle with Sunderland it was his only Division II goal in a seventeen-year career. Sunderland had to wait until the following season for their promotion as a result of Harmer's goal.

When West Ham signed Dudley Tyler in 1972 from Hereford United for £25,000 it was the highest fee paid for a player from a non-League club at that time.

Bob Ferrier, who was born in Sheffield, made the greatest number of appearances in the Scottish League with 626 between 1918 and 1937.

Christmas was particularly happy for Everton's William Cook in 1938 when he scored from the penalty spot in three consecutive matches over the holiday period beginning on Christmas Eve.

When Moussa Balagobin won the football pools he decided to use part of his winnings watching his favourite club, Manchester City. In Moussa's case this involved a trip of 6,000 miles from his Indian Ocean home of Mauritius. His arrival at the game was delayed by a week that he spent in Pentonville while immigration officers checked that he was not an illegal immigrant. His devotion was rewarded by Joe Mercer who gave him a complimentary ticket for their next match against Spurs at White Hart Lane.

In 1970 West Germany's star plàyer Uwe Seeler played his twenty-first and last World Cup finals match.

On Christmas Day 1940 Tommy Lawton and Ken Shackleton both played in two different Football League matches in the same day. Lawton played for Everton against Liverpool in the morning and played as a guest for Tranmere against Crewe in the afternoon, while Shackleton played for the two Bradford clubs, his own, Park Avenue, in the morning and Bradford City in the afternoon.

On the same day in a Wartime League (South) match Brighton arrived to play Norwich with only five men. They asked some spectators to make up their side and lost 0–18.

The record attendance for any Southern League match was set on Christmas Day 1907 when 27,786 spectators watched the match between Queen's Park Rangers and Plymouth Argyle.

On Boxing Day 1935 Tranmere Rovers beat Oldham Athletic 13–4 in a Division III (North) match to set up a record of seventeen goals scored in a Football League match.

Luton were leading Northampton 5–0 at half time during their Boxing Day match in Division III (South) in 1927. Perhaps too much of the Christmas spirit overcame them during half-time, because when play resumed Northampton struck back and left the field the winners by six goals to five.

On Boxing Day 1932 J. Oakes played for Port Vale in their Division II match with Charlton Athletic. Bad light forced the game to be abandoned before full time and by the time the re-arranged fixture was played Oakes found himself playing for 'the other side', having been transferred to Charlton between the two matches.

'Anyone fancy a game of football?'

27

John Charles, who was born in Swansea on 27 December 1931, won the Italian Footballer of the Year award in 1958.

Between 1924 and 1926 there was a Scottish League Division III that was won by Arthurlie in 1924, Nithsdale Wanderers in 1925, and Helensburgh in 1926.

Lord Kinnaird won five FA Cup winners' medals, with the Wanderers in 1873, 1877 and 1878 and with the Old Etonians in 1879 and 1882.

Writing in the *Guardian*, Albert Barham carried the heading 'Queen in brawl at Palace' over his report of a game that included some antics by Crystal Palace's Gerry Queen on his home ground at Selhurst Park.

28

Southampton's 11–0 victory over Northampton Town in the Southern League on 28 December 1901 is still the highest win in the club's history.

Bury reputedly got the nickname the Shakers from a remark made by their chairman in 1891. When asked about team changes for a match against what was believed to be a stronger side, his reply was 'We'll shake them' — and the name has stuck.

In 1958 Raith Rovers became the first Scottish League club to run a lottery.

Laurie Blyth, who played for Glasgow Rangers between 1951 and 1953, is the only known Catholic to have played for this traditionally Protestant club since the end of the Second World War.

Forty-two football matches in the Football League, FA Cup, Scottish League and Scottish Cup programmes were cancelled because of severe weather on 29 December 1962.

When Bolton Wanderers won the FA Cup in 1926 only one member of the team, Greenhalgh, had no previous FA Cup final experience.

Billy Steel was picked to play for Scotland after playing in only seven League matches for Morton in 1946.

Danny Blanchflower is one of the few personalities to have refused to be the surprise subject on *This Is Your Life*.

Colchester United recorded their greatest win on 30 December 1961 when they beat Bradford City 9–1 in their Division IV match.

The Brazilian internationals Carringha and Jairzino won 141 caps between them and both wore the number seven shirt to win the Brazilian League championships for Botafogo.

Arthur Rowley, who holds the record for the greatest number of goals scored in League matches, also holds records at Leicester City for forty-four goals scored in a season, and at Shrewsbury Town for a total of 152 goals from his time with the club as its player-manager in 1958/59, as well as the club's goal-scoring record for one season which he set at thirty-eight.

Between December 1883 and December 1886 Blackburn Rovers went for a record run of twenty-four FA cup ties without a defeat.

In 1974 Brierley's sponsored Peterborough United for £5,000 in an FA Cup tie with Leeds. At the time it was the highest ever sponsorship fee.

Queen's Park Rangers had four managers within three months in the 1968/69 season: Alec Stock, Bill Dodgin, Tommy Docherty and Les Allen.

Wembley Stadium was built on the site of Watkin's Folly, a large steel tower which had been erected by Sir Edward Watkins, a former chairman of the Metropolitan Railway.

The programme 'Sports Special' that preceded *Match of the Day* used to begin with a sequence in which a tall, commanding player broke from his penalty area, ran the length of the pitch and made an easy goal for a colleague. The player featured in that sequence was John Charles, playing for Wales against England at Cardiff.

In 1980 Arsenal reached their eleventh FA Cup final to equal the record set by Newcastle, though Arsenal played all their matches at Wembley.

The first time that floodlights were used in a full international at Wembley was when England drew 1-1 with Spain in 1955.

Ian Edwards came on as substitute for Wales in his first full international game during their 1978 match with Malta and scored four goals in their 7-0 victory.

Orjan Persson, a Swedish international of the 1960s, won three of his eleven caps while attached to Dundee United in 1964.

The National Playing Fields Association

The National Playing Fields Association is an independent charity with a Royal Charter devoted to the preservation, improvement and acquisition of playing fields, playgrounds and play space where they are most needed and for those who need them most, in particular children, young people and the handicapped.

When the Association was founded, in 1925, land was relatively easy to obtain. Today the demand for land is creating a dangerous and growing threat to recreational spaces of all sorts. It is a threat the National Playing Fields Association is here to resist.

Every year some 11,500 children are fatally or seriously injured and approximately 500 children are killed in road accidents. Children and young people depend on adults to provide play and recreational opportunities and they are being let down. The National Playing Fields Association recognizes that play is vital to a child's development. A child who cannot play is seriously deprived.

The charity's main concern has always been with the recreational needs of children and young people. How important are these? In positive terms, proper provision for children is basic to their healthy development. Lack of play and safe recreational opportunities can lead to loneliness, frustration, boredom, vandalism and crime.

After sixty years this message taken from the first page of the first annual report of the National Playing Fields Association still applies:

> The keeping of very small children off the streets by providing for them in congested areas small playgrounds where there is no risk of injury by motor or other wheeled traffic; and secondly, the provision of adequate playing fields for the masses of young people who, having no room themselves to play, rush in thousands to look on at others playing, or perhaps indulge in less desirable pursuits.

It always costs money to do something. It will cost us much more if we do nothing.

Goaldiggers

For children, play is not a trivial pastime — but a means whereby they develop towards physical, mental, emotional and social security.

Without somewhere safe to play, a child is seriously deprived. The Goaldiggers came into being with one simple aim — to help provide hard surface play areas where children can — among other activities — kick a ball about in safety

It is as simple — and as important — as that.

In the last twelve years or so, the Goaldiggers Trust has given grants of over £250,000. It could do so much more — if it had more at its disposal.

The Goaldiggers Club exists to raise money for the Trust through fund-raising events — this book is one such fund-raiser. The proceeds will go towards helping more children to benefit from safe play areas — a simple aim, but such a worthwhile one!

If you would like to help us or like to know more about the work of Goaldiggers and the National Playing Fields Association please write to me:

Jimmy Hill
25 OVINGTON SQUARE
LONDON SW3 1LQ